William Yang

William Yang founded Tabor House in 1990. It was the first centre in the Netherlands that offered psycho-spiritual counselling and support to cancer patients and their relatives. Drawing on spiritual traditions from East and West, he aims to integrate different modes of meditation and psycho-energetic exercises as an essential part of the therapeutic process. The results of his study on the existential crisis among cancer patients were first published in *Existential Crisis and the Awareness of Dying: The Role of Meaning and Spirituality* (2010).

In later years, he researched the interconnection between changes in the experience of the body and in a person's perspective on life and the sense of self. Through his doctoral research, William uncovered a dimension of a truly lived and embodied spirituality, resulting in a heightened process of individuation.

Ton Staps

Ton Staps is a health psychologist and psychotherapist who, from 1976–1998, worked as a staff member in the Department of Medical Psychology at the University Medical Centre of Radboud University in Nijmegen, the Netherlands. As a psychologist, he worked for the department of radiation therapy, where he counselled and supported many cancer patients. He held a teaching position in the faculty of medicine.

When Tabor House was founded in 1990, Ton was very much present, offering his expertise as a supervisor of the team and contributing to the work across different functions over many years. He worked as a senior researcher in Tabor House and participated in a qualitative research project which focused on the changing experience of the body in the process of dealing with an existential crisis.

William Yang

LOSING ME, BECOMING ME

Developing a vision of a lived and embodied spirituality based on experience of people with cancer

AUSTIN MACAULEY PUBLISHERS™

LONDON * CAMBRIDGE * NEW YORK * SHARJAH

A CIP catalogue record for this title is available from the British Library.

ISBN 9781035819164 (Paperback)
ISBN 9781035819171 (ePub e-book)

www.austinmacauley.co.uk

First Published 2024
Austin Macauley Publishers Ltd®
1 Canada Square
Canary Wharf
London
E14 5AA

At the heart of this book are the voices of the many cancer patients who shared with us their most intimate moments of hope and despair, fear and joy. They are too many to name individually, but we are greatly indebted to all of them. They have been our true teachers in developing the ideas that are expounded in this book. Struggling with a life-threatening disease means far more than dealing with a medical diagnosis. At a very profound level, it involves a psycho-spiritual process, an authentic form of a truly lived and embodied spirituality. Cancer patients can show us what it means to learn to live in the midst of the paradoxes of life and death. We hope this book does justice to their humanity, vulnerability and courageous struggle.

We also want to thank our colleagues at Tabor House. For more than 20 years, we were travellers along the same path. We were a warm and learning community, sharing with each other how we were touched and moved in our daily contacts with the patients and their loved ones. We were fortunate that for a long time, we could do this in that wonderful place we called 'our' Tabor House. Patients would often say that they already started to feel different when they stepped out of the car and made their way to the house as if some kind of warmth and radiance embraced them.

When William started to translate the Dutch text into English, he met—through a good friend, Leonie Mak—Susan Verkerk-Wheatley. Prior to their first meeting, he understood that she had already read the Dutch text, which resonated with her own experience of being a cancer patient. Working with Susan meant that William was able to revisit the work we had done and refine it. Susan helped to make the text more accessible to those interested in uncovering the deeper dimensions of the existential struggle with cancer. In her beautiful and fluent language, the essence of the book came more to the fore and the title for the English text emerged: 'Losing me, Becoming me'. It was inspiring to work with such an intelligent, insightful and attentive translator and reader.

Ultimately, this book gives an insight into the 'condition humaine', that awe-inspiring, challenging and never-ending process of 'Losing Me, Becoming Me'—which concerns us all, whether sick or healthy.

I would like to thank Hennita Jaspers, who is the artist of the image on the front of the book.

William Yang
Ton Staps

Table of Contents

Foreword   **9**

Introduction   **11**

**Part One: Dealing with a Life-Threatening Disease as an Embodied
      Spirituality**   **15**

Chapter One: The Beginning of the Journey   *17*

*Chapter Two: Dramatic Changes in the Experience of the Body, Sense
            of Reality and Self*   *25*

*Chapter Three: The Body as an Instrument, The Body as a Space of
            Experience*   *46*

*Chapter Four: Moments of Transition and Experience of
            Transcendence*   *53*

**Part Two: Three Perspectives of Existential Phenomenology,
      Qi Gong and Hesychasm**   **67**

*Chapter Five: Looking at Patients' Experiences Through Existential
            Phenomenology*   *69*

Chapter Six: The Perspective of Qi Gong   *76*

Chapter Seven: The Perspective of Hesychasm   *95*

Part Three: Towards a Vision of a Lived and Embodied Spirituality   **117**

*Chapter Eight: Experiences of the Patients Viewed from the Perspectives
            of Existential Phenomenology, Qi Gong
            and Hesychasm*   *119*

Chapter Nine: Centring and Trans-Centring: A-Body Oriented Vision
of Lived Spirituality   *129*

Our Vision Visualised in the Icon of the Transfiguration   *146*

Relevance of this Research to the Fields of Cancer Care and Christian
Spirituality   *149*

Appendix Psycho-Energetic Bodywork   **152**

Bibliography   **161**

Foreword

This book sets out a vision for dealing with cancer as a process of lived and embodied spirituality.[1] It is a vision that is rooted in the work of William Yang and Ton Staps. Ton was a psychologist and psychotherapist working with many cancer patients within the radiotherapy department at Radboud Hospital in Nijmegen.

William worked as a psycho-energetic therapist at the Canisius-Wilhelmina Hospital, Nijmegen, where he provided psycho-social support for people with cancer. Together with a number of their colleagues, they initiated Tabor House, the first centre in the Netherlands that provided psycho-spiritual support to patients with cancer and other life-threatening illnesses. The therapy which William and Ton developed during their work in two Nijmegen hospitals lent a special character to the support and guidance provided at Tabor House.

Throughout their partnership William and Ton developed and refined the body-based psycho-spiritual practices used at Tabor House, grounding them in scientific research. In Tabor House, patients spoke about existential themes of human existence, such as the loss of life's meaning and the struggle to rediscover it, the deep loneliness and longing for social connection, the loss of social status and the drive to maintain or regain self-respect and personal dignity.

These themes also challenge those who care for and help patients because they also need to come to terms with the reality of life and death. Patients and caregivers stand as equals, side by side, although patients are often ahead of their caregivers when it comes to struggling with these issues. When the meaning of life itself is in jeopardy, the spiritual journey involves peering into the depths of human existence and discovering in there signs of new life.

---

[1] The term 'lived spirituality' and 'embodied spirituality' are often used in conjunction with each other. Towards the end of this book the word embodied spirituality is increasingly accentuated.

Through their work Ton and William were able to discern moments of darkness and light. Patients not only spoke about sublime and elevated states of being but of struggle. They were engaged in a process of learning to face 'Reality-as-it-is'. This Reality is often dramatically different to what patients anticipate and imagine. Having a life-threatening disease such as cancer encompasses a whole range of both terrible and wonderful experiences. It takes people into a 'mysterium fascinans et tremendum',[2] a fascinating and terrifying mystery. This is why, in this book, Reality is written with an initial capital letter.

The results of years of collaborative working and research culminated in William being awarded a doctorate by Radboud University in Nijmegen, the Netherlands.[3] The book you are holding attempts to make that research accessible to a wider English-speaking audience. It does not include the detailed rationale, methodology and research sources which form an integral part of a scientific thesis but does include some of the theoretical background to the research. It aims to take you on a journey into a vision of spirituality which is grounded in the Reality of what is.

---

[2] Otto, R. (1932) *Das Heilige: über das Irrationale in der Idee des Göttlichen und sein Verhältnis zum Rationalen*, 11th edition, Stuttgart/Gotha: Verlag Friedrich Andres Perthes, 34.

[3] W. Yang, *'Begrensd en ont-grensd', Paradoxen in de veranderende beleving van het lichaam bij kanker en een geleefde spiritualiteit,* (Nijmegen: Valkhof Pers, 2018). William's PhD is available in a digital version at: http://hdl.handle.net/2066/197386. A Dutch version of the PhD written for a wider audience is available under the title *Ontworden om te worden wie je bent.* Ton Staps en William Yang (Nijmegen|, Valkhof Pers, 2019).

Introduction

This book *Losing me, Becoming me* is about a lived and embodied form of spirituality, uncovered and developed over many years of listening attentively to the voices and experiences of cancer patients. These were 'ordinary' people facing 'extraordinary' circumstances. This book explores the human search for meaning during a time of profound confrontation with human vulnerability and mortality.

Losing me, Becoming me is not a theoretical treatise about the relationship between body and mind. Rather, it stresses the urgent need for a discourse on spirituality which does not attempt to disentangle body, mind and soul, often subjugating the body. It is not a form of spirituality which aspires to transcend human immanence for the sake of some transcendent realm beyond human physical existence. *Losing me, Becoming me* is a book which argues passionately for the need to embrace all that we are, through a compassionate, deeply empathic and tender stance towards the reality that we are *embodied* beings.

The ideas explored in this book are derived from many years of working with cancer patients. It goes without saying that, when it comes to a life-threatening disease such as cancer, the body cannot be ignored. In virtually every hour of the day and night, the body makes itself felt. It cries out to be acknowledged, taken care of, accepted as-it-is, despite its dire predicament. Living with cancer involves a profound journey of deep crisis and transformation, in and through experiences such as a 'dark night', impasse, resistance and also unexpected moments of inner light, dazzling sparks illuminating the darkness.

People with cancer confront us with the reality that we are vulnerable, mortal beings. What is happening to them today may happen to us tomorrow and to those we love. By listening to the voices and experiences of cancer patients, we might also learn more about what it means to navigate our way through those times of profound human bewilderment, storm-ravaged periods of life when our roadmap is torn apart in front of us.

When listening to the experiences of cancer patients, you will often hear them wrestling with the precarious relationship between body and mind, the body-mind split which, for centuries, has pervaded much of Western culture. This split has also led to a distortion of the Christian message, which is fundamentally about immanence *and* transcendence; the cross *and* the mystery of resurrection!

Neo-Platonism pushed early Christianity towards a deep body-mind (spirit) dichotomy in which the body was seen, in Plato's words, as the 'dungeon of the spirit'. The spirit needed to be liberated from the shackles of the body, which was thought to be the breeding ground of everything that was bad and evil: sickness, sin, malice and lust.

This animosity towards the body points to a profound woundedness in our thinking and the way we live in the Western world today. This is the spiritual-cultural heritage we have been born into and it has impacted on the way we (dis)connect with our body. It governs how we view ourselves in relation to wider creation, that body we often call Mother Earth. We see the consequence of this disconnection unfolding right before our eyes, in the ecological disaster of our time.

People with cancer not only suffer from the predicament of their illness but also from having to face the deep woundedness of this mind-body split. A diagnosis of cancer can mean a painful confrontation with how we view our body. Before being diagnosed with a life-threatening disease such as cancer, we may simply think of it as an instrument, a vehicle through which we function in the world.

The crisis of a cancer diagnosis and the treatment which this involves can often mean having to reconnect with the body, viewing it less as an instrument and more as a sensory-sensitive living entity. *Losing me, Becoming me* attempts to describe this journey.

This book is a testimony to the many challenging and profoundly insightful words and experiences which patients have shared over the years. By listening attentively to the way in which they describe their experiences, it is possible to gain insight into the way the body is experienced before, during and after illness. These changes impact strongly on how they look at the reality of life and death and how they see themselves as a person.

This book aims to explore two fundamental dimensions of human existence: the perspective of 'Reality-as-it-is' and the experience of self, as the person one is. These two dimensions lie at the heart of an authentic and embodied spirituality.

This book has been divided into three parts:

Part One begins with the existential crisis when people lose their hold on life, its meaning and their sense of self. In the world of spirituality, this is often called the 'Dark Night of the Soul'. The journey through any 'dark night' is often spoken of as if it is a purely spiritual experience when, in reality, all spirituality is experienced in and through the body. Three philosophical/spiritual traditions are introduced in which the body is of crucial importance, namely: existential phenomenology, Qi Gong and hesychasm.

These three perspectives help to throw light on the depth of the experiences of cancer patients which the ordinary Western mind can find hard to comprehend. In Chapter Two, the voices of cancer patients begin to be heard. They speak about how they experience the changes in their body and the impact these have on their view of Reality and sense of Self. These changes are 'mapped' against the four stages of the illness.

Chapter Three delves more deeply into how the body is experienced in the four stages of the illness and it distinguishes on a somewhat more abstract level between a *functional-instrumental* and a *sensory-sensitive* experience of the body. In Chapter Four, we look more closely at some remarkable cross-border experiences of a number of our patients. Especially those who participated in a programme of psycho-energetic bodywork. Three important key concepts come to the fore: incarnation, centring and transcendence. These concepts lie at the heart of the vision of an embodied spirituality, which is the focus of this book.

Part Two explores at a deeper level the three perspectives of existential phenomenology, Qi Gong and hesychasm. These perspectives offer different and interesting windows for looking at the concepts of incarnation, centring and transcendence. Chapter Five focuses on existential phenomenology, which provides a window for viewing the confrontation with death and the finiteness of life. Chapter Six enters the world of Qi Gong, a Chinese spiritual practice through which people experience themselves as part of a greater whole, of nature and the cosmos. Chapter Seven explores hesychasm, an early Christian mystical tradition, which provides a way of holding together the finite and the infinite, the mortal and immortal, the human and divine. Part Two leads into the development of a vision of a lived and embodied spirituality, as explored in Part Three.

Part Three sets out the vision towards a lived and embodied spirituality. Chapter Eight explicitly makes the links between the three perspectives of existential phenomenology, Qi Gong and hesychasm and the experience of the patients. Chapter Nine introduces and explores the novel concept of trans-centring, in which the paradox between incarnation and transcendence is reconciled. The newly introduced term 'trans-centring' forms the bridge, the connecting link, between the material mundane level of life and the immaterial, transcendent level.

The book concludes with a reflection on the icon of the Transfiguration of Jesus Christ on Mount Tabor as a blueprint for the human person. The icon makes visible that every human being lives within a concrete, horizontal-immanent reality without being limited by this.

At the same time, human beings are also part of a transcendent reality without being dissolved into this. They live simultaneously within a horizontal-immanent and vertical-transcendent reality. Embodied spirituality is ultimately about becoming 'who you really are'. The ultimate perspective here is to become a *person,* within whom are integrated two seemingly opposite dimensions: the immanent and transcendent, the human and divine.

Part One
Dealing with a Life-Threatening Disease
as an Embodied Spirituality

Chapter One
The Beginning of the Journey

The existential crisis as a present day 'dark night of the soul'.

Losing me

In sixteenth century literature on 'spirituality', much is written about the Dark Night of the Soul.[4] This is the moment when all meaning of life and faith in God are completely lost.

Today, patients with cancer experience a more profane, but no less real dark night. It was 'as if the whole world collapsed around me' or 'as if the floor sank away from underneath my feet', is how some cancer patients describe this moment. Patients tend to be rather reticent in speaking about this moment. It is as if words either cannot capture the depth of this experience or they feel ashamed to have fallen so deeply into despair and hopelessness. The reticence might also be because they fear that speaking about the experience may also mean reviving and reliving it.

When listening to the voices of cancer patients, our first focus tended to be on the existential crisis and the so-called 'dark night' and not on the precarious relationship between body and mind. It is important for cancer patients to first give voice to the experience of their dark night. Listening to their experiences made it possible to discover the defining aspects of the 'dark night' and what constitutes its 'essential nature'.

It is important to acknowledge and respect that the confrontation with the dark night poses a profound psycho-spiritual challenge and that it should not be

---

[4] St. John of the Cross, *The Dark Night,* translated by Kieran Kavanaugh, O.C.D and Otilia Rodriquez, O.C.D., (Washington D.C., Institute of Carmelite Studies, 1973), 297–388.

judged too soon as a psychological, even psychiatric disturbance. Cancer patients are not psychologically disturbed. Like all of us, they struggle to discover the meaning of life and to make sense of who they are. It is in understanding this that we can open the way to a renewed sense of human dignity and self-esteem.

Defining aspects of an existential crisis and its essential nature

During the many years of listening to the voices of cancer patients[5] we were able to uncover seven main aspects which characterise an existential crisis:

Awareness of finiteness

"When I heard I had cancer, it felt to me like a death sentence. The possibility of dying one day suddenly became an irrevocable reality." (Man, age 54)

The acute awareness of finiteness, the realisation that death is not something that happens in a distant future but can be imminent, proved to be the main characteristic of the existential crisis. This awareness of finiteness not only occurs on hearing the diagnosis but at any moment during the course of the disease.

Dissolution of the future

"The cancer was like a chopping knife that cut me off from the rest of my life." (Woman, age 50)

Until that moment, the time for living seems to be endless. Death is far off, beyond a far horizon. The future suddenly becomes very limited and restricted. What remains of the future appears threatening and alarming.

Loss of purpose and meaning

"And the next moment, one wonders what's the use of me being here? Why am I still here?" (Woman, age 50)

_____

[5] We embarked on a small scale qualitative research project which involved extensive interviews (with 13 patients), analyzing written answers to open-ended questions (from 58 patients) and autobiographical reading of a couple of patients. (Use was also made of filmed interviews from an earlier DVD: *When the Mirror Breaks*.[5])

Being faced with a limited life expectancy disrupts the whole life plan. Goals that give direction to life, certainly in the long-term, now lose their meaning. There is a sense that future aspirations will no longer be reached. Our life shared with loved ones may have to be relinquished. Long-held religious and philosophical beliefs come to be questioned.

Severe emotional distress: fear, anxiety, panic, despair

"I panicked completely. I thought I was going crazy." (Man, age 56)

Many patients fully realise the threats that await them in the future. What people had heard previously about cancer, especially what is negative, is now activated and evokes severe feelings of fear, panic and despair.

Loneliness

"At that moment, I consciously realised that I was alone, that I had to go through it all by myself, despite all the love and care that I felt around me." (Woman, age 51)

Many patients suddenly experience themselves as an outsider, 'marked by fate' by a deadly disease. They no longer feel part of the community of normal healthy people.

Powerlessness

"I thought: I can't handle this. What I felt was powerlessness. This is too much, too big, too ..." (woman, age 51)

Faced with the disease, patients feel powerless. They do not recognise the intensity of the feelings they now experience and feel powerless to repress or cope with them.

Identity crisis

"At that moment, my whole life and personality coincided with having cancer." (Woman, age 50)

How people see themselves in terms of their identity is thrown into turmoil. Questions arise about the sense of self. Who am I? What is left of me? What good can I now do? This loss of the familiar sense of self, of a trusted identity, can be aggravated by a physical mutilation of the body and dependency on others.

Of the above aspects, the first four are about the perspective on Reality-as-it-is, the last three with the sense of Self. This means that the essential nature of an existential crisis can be subsumed under just two categories: perspective of Reality and sense of Self.

We discovered that patients deal with an existential crisis in different ways. Some patients cannot find a way out of their crisis. They seem to get stuck, trapped in one of the feelings we described above: despair, powerlessness, sadness. Others find a way of enduring and dealing with this crisis in their existence. This can be a profoundly challenging and yet, at the same time, deeply creative and authentic spiritual process.

Uncovering the spiritual dimension in dealing with an existential crisis.

Becoming me

It is the journey through the dark night of an existential crisis that becomes the focus of the next step. The main question now is whether there is a spiritual dimension in dealing with this crisis? And if there is one, then what character would it have? Does it offer a deeper perspective on spirituality, one that is not only meaningful for people with cancer but for all other mortal human beings as well?

Spirituality as a process of fundamental change

There are many descriptions and definitions of spirituality. We heard patients speak about how their lives had fundamentally changed after receiving the diagnosis of cancer, especially regarding their outlook on life and the way they saw themselves as a person. Or in the terms described earlier: their perspective on Reality and the sense of Self.

Hearing cancer patients describe profound experiences in body, mind and soul opened the way to investigate further the spiritual dimension of the journey through an existential crisis and what it means to cope with a life-threatening disease. It was fascinating to see how far-reaching the changes were between the period before and after the illness. In comparing these periods, it became clear that truly fundamental changes had taken place in how the patients related to 'Reality-as-it-is', as well as how they experienced their sense of 'Self'.[6]

It became clear that dealing with an existential crisis involves a process of inner transformation, with many ups and downs. In this context, it is clear that spirituality should not be identified with a firm belief in a God above or some elevated, extraordinary experience of meaning. Rather, it involves a process that includes periods where even the meaning of life is lost altogether, causing deep pain and bewilderment. We, therefore, consider the 'dark night of the soul', which marked the beginning of our study, to be an integral part of this process.

On the other hand, we discovered that unexpected moments could also occur when new meaning breaks through and life is once again embraced and cherished. The spiritual challenge involves learning to accept and integrate these moments of light and darkness, the loss of all meaning in life and the unexpected gift of a new perspective on life … and death.

We also discovered that patients were tossed back and forth between extremely contradictory thoughts and feelings, hope and despair, resistance and surrender. Spirituality, grounded in the lives of ordinary people who find themselves in sometimes extraordinary situations, is a very dynamic and truly 'dialectical' process, one in which strongly conflicting polarities need to be accepted and reconciled.

The crucial role of the body in the spiritual process.

Finally having become myself

The confrontation with a life-threatening disease in one's own body not only provokes an existential crisis, but it also intensifies this when the disease progresses and physical complaints during treatments are increasingly and painfully felt. However, the body is also indispensable as a channel for feeling, expressing and processing emotions (essential in the grieving process). The body is also crucial in bringing the focus of attention back to the present, the here-and-

---

[6] See also: Yang, W., Staps, T. and Hijmans, E. (2012) 'Going through a Dark Night: Existential Crisis in Cancer Patients—Effective Coping as a Psycho-spiritual Process embedded in the Vulnerability of the Body', *Studies in Spirituality*, 22, 311–339.

now. Whilst our minds can end up constantly thinking about and getting lost in many fears about the future, the body can only be present in the here-and-now.

Once a patient has regained contact with his or her body and again feels at home in it, then it can become the place for discovering new meaning, the means by which the world can be viewed with new eyes. This is beautifully expressed by a man who was diagnosed with an incurable lung cancer:

"… and so I went out again for the first time to take a walk. At one moment, I found myself asking: what is it that I'm seeing over there? It was the outline of a tree. But it was so new to me! I was overwhelmed by seeing something that was so new and which I could name. It was incredible. I was able to say: it's a tree!" (man, 56 years)

Here is someone speaking about a new perspective on reality, a new sense of who he is and the way he looks at the world around him. In listening to this man and also to other cancer patients, we heard many fascinating and often moving stories that gave us a deeper insight into the connection between the experiences of the body and the outlook on life and the sense of self.[7] Whilst listening to these stories we heard pointers to key elements which constitute a lived and embodied spirituality, a spirituality that is grounded in daily life and the human body.

---

[7] We began a new qualitative study and conducted a second series (round) of in-depth interviews. We used thirty of these interviews to form three different groups of ten people which could then be compared.

Group 1 was made up of ten patients who had taken part in the full programme offered at Tabor House. The programme consisted of individual counselling, psycho-energetic bodywork in a group and individual haptonomic massage treatments.[7] Patients were selected who had completed their medical treatment and the Tabor House programme approximately five years previously. These were also patients who continued working on a daily basis with the psycho-energetic bodywork. The prognosis for the majority of these patients had been considered to be negative or very uncertain.

Group 2 was made up of ten patients who had only recently started their counselling programme at Tabor House. At the time of the interviews they had taken part in a basic psycho-energetic bodywork programme of six, two-hour sessions. Almost all of these patients were still undergoing medical treatment. Within this group the perspectives on the outcome of their medical treatment varied widely.

Group 3 was made up of ten patients who had not received some form of counselling. These were patients who had completed their medical treatment approximately five years previously.

On hearing the stories of the patients and trying to understand them, we related their experiences to three culturally and historically divergent traditions that deal with existential questions concerning body and mind and life and death, namely: existential phenomenology, Qi Gong and hesychasm. They provide a rich and challenging framework for valuing and interpreting the experiences of patients.

1. Existential phenomenology, a Western philosophical movement which flourished in the mid-twentieth century and explicitly acknowledges the finite nature of human life.
2. The practice of Qi Gong, embedded in Chinese Daoism, which views the human being as an integral part of nature and the infinite cosmos.
3. The practice of hesychasm, rooted in Eastern Orthodox Christianity, which offers a perspective on the finiteness of the human being within the infinite.

At the heart of all three traditions is the significance assigned to the body, its psychological and spiritual transformations and how these are experienced. They deal with the relationship between body and mind and offer perspectives for overcoming the dualism which often characterises this relationship in Western culture. Existential phenomenology offers an explicitly atheistic perspective on life, whilst Qi Gong looks at it from a basically non-theistic viewpoint and hesychasm from an explicitly theistic one.

We found it especially interesting to discover the focus which hesychasm gives to the body, something that has often been neglected in Christian teaching, despite the fact that Christ was God incarnate and was crucified and resurrected in his body. Within Eastern Orthodox theology, the relationship between body and mind is a central theme. The incarnation of Jesus Christ, a basic tenet in all Christian belief, means ultimately recognising and appreciating the body and all material reality.

In fact, it was this tenet, surrounding the reality of Christ's body that was fiercely debated during the Council of Chalcedon, held in the year 453.[8] The

---

[8] Theologians who have re-thought the dogma of Chalcedon include Karl Rahner, Walter Kasper, Edward Schillebeeckx, Piet Schoonenberg and Wolfhart Pannenberg. See also Rahner, K., Grillmeier, A. and Bacht, H. (Eds) (1954) "Chalkedon—Ende oder Anfang?", *Das Konzil von Chalkedon,* vol. 3. Würzburg: Echter Verlag.

relevance of this study on an embodied spirituality among patients struggling with the reality of their bodies should be viewed against the background of this broader cultural-historic and spiritual-religious context.

Chapter Two
Dramatic Changes in the Experience of the Body, Sense of Reality and Self

In this chapter, we describe the changes which the cancer patients experienced in their bodies and how these often dramatically differed during different stages of their illness.[9]

As we attempt to tell the story of these shifts and changes, we include the words that the patients shared with us. We describe how the physical changes which the patients experienced during their illness also impacted on the way they viewed the Reality of their life and how they experienced the Self. In mapping these changes during the different stages, we were able to discover the significant elements of an embodied spirituality. To try to get a picture of this, we divided the process of living with a life-threatening disease into four stages:

Stage 1: Life with a healthy body before the disease.
Stage 2: The moment during and shortly after diagnosis.
Stage 3: The period of medical treatment.
Stage 4: Five years after medical treatment.

For each stage, we describe the changes in the experience of the body and the connection with these, the changes in the view of Reality and the sense of Self. We end each stage with a short description of those elements which we think characterise an embodied and lived spirituality.

---

[9] In this chapter, we look at the experiences of the patients in the three research groups as a whole. We did not therefore distinguish between these different groups. We found remarkable differences between the groups, in particular between the groups that did/did not receive psycho-social support at Tabor House. This is discussed in Chapter Four.

Stage 1: The naïve, 'unsuspecting body'

hoc erat corpus meum (this was my body)

The experience of the body before the disease

The way in which the patients experienced their healthy body before the onset of disease contrasted sharply with how they experienced it after diagnosis. It was against the background of having a previously healthy and fit body that the changes occurring during the disease process stood out more clearly. Before the life-threatening illness was diagnosed, the body was experienced in a number of ways.

- *reliable and above suspicion*

The patients we interviewed said that before they became ill, they actively focused on achieving goals and living a pleasant, meaningful and successful life. For them, their body was the 'instrument' through which these goals should be achieved. The simple, non-functional and non-goal-oriented 'enjoyment' of the body was reserved for those moments of relaxation, such as during the evening, weekends and holidays. These were the times when people could recover from having worked hard and build up new energy reserves in order to return to work.

Most of the patients we interviewed said that before they became ill, they were generally 'comfortable in their skin' and had enough energy to do what they wanted. They perceived their body as something which was reliable and above suspicion.

- *inexhaustibly and limitlessly active*

A 52-year-old woman with breast cancer described how she saw herself before her diagnosis: "I was someone who could always do anything. What I wanted I did and I managed OK. I could do ten things all at once. I studied, I worked and could pull it all together."

A young man aged 32 with chronic lymphocytic leukaemia described his life before his illness: "We were regularly asked to work overtime or to get something done at short notice. That was never a problem for me. I've always been active, always worked, never took things easy and was never really able to just sit down." Other patients also said: "It was just the way it was with my body, it could simply do anything I wanted!"

From the way these patients spoke about their body before the disease, it seems that there were no limits to doing what they wanted. This boundlessness is somehow evident in the recurring use of words such as 'always', 'everything' and 'never'.

- *self-evident and unconscious*

The recurrent use of words such as 'always' and 'everything' is striking and gave the impression that the patients were not really aware of physical boundaries and limits to their energy levels. The healthy body tended to be viewed as possessing an inexhaustible source of energy, something that was unproblematic. The vitality of the body was so self-evident that patients were not even really conscious of their body.

For example, a man of 65, who had a cancerous growth in the lung (small cell lung cancer), said: "I was hardly aware of my body. There was nothing wrong with me. Everything was simply as it appeared to be."

- *an instrument of direction and control*

Given that the body was perceived as an instrument for achieving their goals and possessing inexhaustible supplies of energy, the patients believed that they could lead and direct their lives as they wished and that everything was 'under control'. This belief was so taken for granted that one woman said: "If you live your life in the right way, nothing detrimental can happen to you." (Woman, 52 years, breast cancer)

What she meant was that the control which could be exerted over the body extended to such an extent that she was able to prevent the disease from happening—that death could be kept at a safe distance.

- *and yet, there are limits! Learning the hard way in the school of life*

We also talked with patients who had encountered physical limitations at some point in their lives. The body, which functioned as a willing instrument and

27

load carrier for a long time, eventually made itself felt, sometimes with annoying, but persistent complaints. Bodily ailments and complaints confronted them with the hard fact that limits do indeed exist. These limits propelled them into the hard reality of life, forcing them to take their body more seriously. However, this does not always mean that they were willing to listen to the signals their body gave.

A patient said: "You have a little tension in your head, pain in your neck, in your muscles and in your back. You think you've just done a little too much, but the tension does not go away. Looking back, I can now see that this was my body telling me to stop and not to keep on going. But I did not listen and then things went too far." (Man, 57 years old, prostate cancer). At a later moment in the interview, this man confessed that after ignoring these complaints, he had experienced burnout.

In some patients, the signals coming from their body were so strong they could not be ignored. They could have been caused by Chronic Fatigue Syndrome, a serious accident or an innate fragile physical condition. The physical signals that accompanied these disorders made it necessary for these patients to accept boundaries which needed to be respected. Even before the disease was diagnosed, these people learned to limit the many activities they were engaged in drastically or to even stop them altogether.

The confrontation with their limitations had initiated a 'learning process' in which space needed to be created for acknowledging the body's vulnerability, for setting limits and for recognising that life is ultimately outside of their control. When these people were later diagnosed with cancer, they continued walking this path.

For example, a woman explained that in learning to cope with the consequences of a car accident, she had learned the importance of maintaining a positive relationship with her body. When this same woman was diagnosed with cancer, she said that the earlier experience of the accident meant that she was gentler towards her body and was able to maintain a positive attitude towards it: "I have to keep loving my body. After all, it can't help being the way it is." (Woman, 63 years old, ovarian cancer)

The patients who were confronted with limitations prior to their illness pointed to the reality that listening to the body and dealing with limits is a lifelong learning process. What they said did show that some of them had learned to deal with limits and limitations earlier in life and were able to draw on this attitude when confronted with a serious illness.

The view of Reality and the experience of Self before the disease

Regarding our patients' view of the Reality of their life and how they saw themselves as persons before the diagnosis of a life-threatening disease, a number of basic characteristics came to the fore, which are described below.

- *life is well-organised and the future predictable*

To begin exploring what we mean by an embodied spirituality, we now describe the connections between the experience of the body before the onset of the disease with the patients' view of Reality and their experience of Self.

For all human beings, life involves continuous change. This means that most of us search for ways of trying to find a sense of meaning and order in the many events of our lives. This search for meaning and order creates a sense of structure and safety by giving us the feeling that we have some control over life. The conviction that the body is somehow reliable and predictable in its functioning forms one of our core beliefs. It is the foundation stone on which our entire system of meaning is constructed, on which life can be organised. The body is simply there without our conscious awareness.

- *the awareness of death is repressed*

Within the meaning system of most people, as was the case in our patients when they were healthy, there is little room for an awareness of finiteness and death. A vivid awareness of human mortality often goes hand-in-hand with a threat of futility and creates an alarming sense of insecurity. By repressing this feeling and projecting death over the horizon into a distant future, we attempt to shield ourselves from this threat and try to prevent our system of meaning from collapsing.

In fact, a framework of meaning in which death is repressed forms the context in which most people live their lives in the Western world today. This repression of death begins at an early age and is deeply ingrained in our minds. This view of life and death can be regarded as the basic cultural frame of reference through which meaning is given or rather *not* given, to finitude and death. The impact of a disease such as cancer needs to be understood against this background.

- *What we learned from this first stage*

In as much as we are able to speak of an embodied spirituality during this stage prior to the illness, it does involve a view of Reality and a sense of Self that is prevalent in the social, cultural environment in which patients are brought up. Within this context, death is repressed. This actually creates an illusory view of reality and sense of self, which connects with the naïve perception of the body as something which is not vulnerable and mortal.

For the majority of our patients, this was indeed the way in which they experienced their body before their sickness. This perception of the body formed the raft on which the entire system of meaning and identity was kept afloat. This unconsciously absorbed and fixed system of ideas about life and death can be seen as something that had become 'congealed' within the body and mind. And yet, this is part and parcel of the process of a 'lived and embodied spirituality', explored later in this book.

Stage 2: The 'damned body'

hoc corpus damnatum est (this body is damned)

The experience of the body at the time of and shortly after diagnosis

For most of the patients, it was a crushing moment when they heard they had cancer. This was certainly the case when the message was completely unexpected, for example, as a result of the so-called preventative medical screening which is carried out across sections of the population.

Before the result, people usually feel well and perceive themselves as belonging to the world of healthy people. The diagnosis of a life-threatening disease is totally at odds with this. It is difficult to accept that the diagnosis is correct. The first reaction can sometimes involve an assumption that a mistake has been made and that the result belongs to someone else. At the moment of hearing the diagnosis or when absorbing the message later on, many of our patients said that they experienced their body in several ways.

- *paralysed and numb*

When the impact of the message actually sunk in, the sense of dismay was great. Whilst often at that time hardly anything had changed physically, patients described feeling 'paralysed' and 'numb'. This was expressed by a man who was diagnosed with lung cancer:

"It didn't matter anymore … The message was too big. I knew I was going to die. Lung cancer! Dead little birdie! It was too much, impossible to comprehend. It's a … death sentence, irrevocable. I was at a total loss, flabbergasted. No emotions at all! They were completely eliminated." (Man, 63 years old, lung cancer)

This man evidently saw his diagnosis as a death sentence. His body had, so to speak, become 'damned'. For this man, the message was so overwhelming that he was unable to connect with it emotionally and was certainly not the only one. Numbness of emotions and paralysis of all activity occurred often among the patients. For example, after hearing that his prostate cancer could not be treated curatively, the man whose words we quoted earlier said:

"At that moment, the world caves in … the whole world is swept away. I fell into a very deep pit. I felt really fucking bad. There was just a dark black haze in front of my eyes. It looked as if I didn't know anything anymore. How do I go on from this point? How long do I have left to live? I felt as though my life had been stolen from me." (Man, 57 years old, prostate cancer)

It took some time before this man was able to think more clearly and to pick up his life again.

- *the body as the very foundation of life falls away*

The men quoted above said little about the way they had experienced their body at the moment of diagnosis. They were not only emotionally numbed but also 'numbed' in the awareness of their body. Yet their body was definitely there and played a crucial role. After all, the diagnosis was about the body that had only recently seemed so reliable and unsuspecting. The body, as the foundation on which life was built, had crumbled. It was this that triggered an existential crisis in many patients, bringing into question the very meaning of their lives and their identity.

31

Dealing with finiteness:
an important lesson in the school of life

We discovered that an existential crisis was not the only response to being diagnosed with cancer. The tendency in many patients was to reduce the threat by assuming that the disease was curable. They were convinced that after the treatment they would be healthy again and able to resume normal life. They focused their attention on the medical treatment and managed not to think too far ahead.

For example, despite having to undergo various painful and complicated operations, a 67-year-old man said: "My horizon was that the doctors were going to fix it. They were going to solve the problem … things did not have to go wrong. I had incredible confidence in those two top surgeons at the hospital." (Man, 67 years old, colon cancer). For this man, being confident of a successful outcome was an effective way of dealing with his illness.

There were also patients, who during their lives had learned to live with the idea of death. Life experience, together with age, can sometimes mean that mortality and death are regarded as an inherent part of life. This became clear in an interview with a Jewish man who had lost many of his relatives in the German concentration camps. He had, from very early on, developed a sense of the vulnerability of life and the reality of death.

However, a professor in one of the exact sciences did not seem to show any signs of an existential crisis. He had a very pragmatic, down-to-earth attitude towards death, which he saw as a fact of life.

These examples show how a framework of meaning, in which the reality of death has a place, can be crucial for dealing with a life-threatening illness. They also show that being more consciously aware of and accepting of the reality that life is finite is something that can be 'learned' through living life as it is, viewing it as part-and-parcel of the school of life.

The view of Reality and the experience of the Self at the time of diagnosis

When it came to how our patients saw the reality of their life and how they experienced their sense of personhood, we found that in this second stage a number of characteristics were present.

- *loss of future: loss of purpose and meaning*

Being confronted with a sense of finiteness did not necessarily occur at the moment of hearing the diagnosis, but it could make itself felt at a later point in time when someone realised that full recovery was not possible. It is at such a moment that death became real. The future was no longer self-evident and the framework of meaning which gave shape and purpose to life was no longer adequate. The taken-for-granted future, the goals, plans and aspirations that nourished the passion for life all began to dissolve into thin air.

The framework of meaning collapsed, as expressed by a woman of 40 years: "And the next day you think what's the use of me being here? Why am I still here in this life?" (Woman, 40 years old, uterine cancer and breast cancer)

The original framework of meaning for most patients proved to be fragile because death had no place in it. Now that death had to be faced, the goals of the past no longer gave direction and meaning to life. "The cancer was like a chopping knife which had cut me off from the rest of my life." (Woman, 52 years old, colon cancer)

The future turned into a black hole. The psychic hold, the framework of meaning that kept everything in its place, had disappeared and intense feelings of fear, despair, sadness and anger were released.

- *loss of identity: powerlessness and loneliness*

Finding themselves in a situation where they were unable to change their physical condition or control the intensity of their own emotions, patients felt helpless: "I thought, I cannot handle all this. What I felt was powerlessness. This is too much, too big, too …" (woman, 53 years old, breast cancer). An additional factor was that the framework of meaning, which was shared with many others, suddenly fell away. This created a sense of being thrown back on the self with a feeling of intense loneliness. Despite all the care and love which other people showed them, patients sometimes felt like outsiders, marked by death: "At that moment I became so aware of how lonely I was. Despite all the love and care which was being shown to me, I had the feeling that I would have to go through this all by myself." (Woman, 53 years old, breast cancer)

Powerlessness and loneliness violated the identity which had been constructed over the course of a lifetime when a person is 'someone' in the eyes of others and had a place in the world: "The moment I heard that I had cancer, my whole life and personality collided with that cancer." (Woman, 52 years old, colon cancer)

Physical mutilation, loss of energy and dependence on others were experienced as an attack on self-esteem and self-respect.

What we learned from this second stage

Being diagnosed with cancer can mean the first and intense confrontation with death. Before this moment, death was something that happened to other people, but now it was a very personal and threatening reality. The former framework of meaning, in which death had no place, had therefore been shattered. Identity, which had been crafted within this framework, was uprooted. The very foundation on which a life had been built, now crumbles. This loss of self might be described by some as a dark night of the soul.

At the end of the description of the first stage, we referred to the culture-based view of Reality, signifying the social-cultural context in which a particular framework of meaning is learned and internalised. The confrontation with death makes it painfully clear how inadequate this framework is.

The struggle with 'Reality-as-it-is' sets a process in motion in which attitudes towards life and death, the meaning of life and existence, have to be redefined. Letting go of ideas and illusions about life is the first step in learning to live life *as it is*. It is in the patients' struggle to come to terms with Reality that spirituality becomes something real and intense. A 'lived', embodied spirituality, is not about 'out of body' exalted states, but an intense process, a wrestling with how life actually is.

Stage 3: The alienated body

Hoc corpus meum est? (is this my body?)

The experience of the body during treatment

The medical treatments, which often involve some combination of surgery, chemotherapy, radiotherapy and hormone therapy, mark the next stage of the disease process. Some patients said that they suffered little from the side effects and were able to endure the treatments quite well. Others found the treatments difficult to bear and this often initiated an existential crisis which hit them only at this time, rather than at the moment of diagnosis. At this stage, the body was experienced in new and powerful ways.

- *a stranger and an enemy*

Whilst at the time of hearing the diagnosis a 'numbness' could be experienced during the time of treatment. However, patients became mercilessly aware of the body through sensations of pain, nausea, fatigue and countless other forms of suffering. For many patients, their own body became a stranger, even an enemy. In the words of a woman treated with chemotherapy for breast cancer:

"From the first chemo, it was disastrous. I was nauseous day and night … I just wanted … to die. My body became a living hell. There it was, this body … that I so desperately wanted to keep and love like nothing else, became at the same time my greatest enemy." (woman, 54 years old, breast cancer)

Another woman also spoke about this sense of alienation from the body, which in her case seemed to have abandoned her completely: "What I found so very difficult was that my body had let me down in this way. You feel healthy, but as you move through the treatment you become more and more sick … which is not really true, because you're undergoing these treatments to get well again!" (Woman, 52 years old, breast cancer)

An additional factor, which adds to the sense of alienation, is the feeling of being 'treated as a patient', being a number in a large and complex medical system and the object of all kinds of standardised medical interventions. Many patients expressed this alienation by saying that they hardly recognised their body as their own because of the side effects of the treatments. They often sighed and said: "Is this still my body?" It was at this stage that the body was experienced as:

- *mercilessly present*

The suffering which arises from the hurt and scarred body during medical treatment means that what is happening in the body cannot be avoided. It is inescapably 'felt' and impossible to ignore. This bodily suffering is accompanied by many painful emotions and triggers intense grief. Grieving is extremely important for processing all that has been lost and for preventing psychological disintegration. It involves accepting the losses, for example, of a healthy physical condition, of having stamina and energy and of a physical integrity, things that are normally taken for granted.

Also, the loss of sexual feelings that occur with certain cancers and their treatments can have a big impact. A man being treated for prostate cancer spoke about this: "My medication is bringing about many changes in my body. I have less hair growth. I am developing small breasts. Feminine things are happening in my body, like hot flushes … Yes, it is my body, but I am bothered by the idea that I can no longer 'do it' … I no longer have the feeling that I really want … because I do not feel anything. I do not get an erection anymore. The desire is not there. In fact, it has completely gone." (Man, 57 years, prostate cancer)

- *a challenge to make peace with the body*

Processing what has invaded their life and their body involved an intense psychic struggle. Patients often felt that they were being thrown back and forth between extreme emotions. Acceptance and resistance, hope and despair, wanting to fight and feeling defeated, all alternated very quickly. This description of being flung 'back and forth' is described by some authors as an *oscillating process*.[10] Nevertheless, many patients were, over time, able to find a psychological balance. For others, this process stagnated and a person was trapped for a long time in a place of revolt, defeat or despair.

Cancer can mean the body becoming a source of misery and pain. It can also mean being challenged to make peace with it, to accept it as it is. Having cancer can therefore mean an opportunity to reconnect with the Self in a true and honest way and to attend to the often powerful emotions that surface during this period of physical and psychological suffering. Being able to express emotions not only means talking about them but also weeping, screaming, even cursing, sighing: "Crying, crying … I still remember it so well. The cry came from the bottom of my heart." (Woman, 51 years old, breast cancer)

Emotions can also be expressed through artwork such as painting, dancing, singing and writing poems.

---

[10] Stroebe, M. S., Schut, H. and Neimeyer, R. (Ed) (2001) 'Meaning Making in the Dual Process of Coping with Bereavement', *Meaning Reconstruction and the Experience of Loss*, Washington: American Psychological Association, 55–73, 58.

It is important that emotions find some form of physical expression and that this is done in a way which is not harmful to the patients and people around them. Expressing emotions can help patients not to end up trapped in fearful and obsessive thoughts about an uncertain and threatening future. It is also by reconnecting with the body that it becomes possible to bring the focus back to the present moment, something which is very important for mental health.

The simple truth is that the body can only be in the here and now, whilst the mind can get lost in panicky thoughts about the future and regrets about the past. We heard a remarkable example of this during the interview with the man with lung cancer whom we quoted earlier. He said: "At that moment, being aware of my breath helped me. Somehow, I managed to keep my attention focused on my breathing. I did not ask myself if I would still be breathing in an hour's time. The fact is that I was breathing … now. There was only breathing: in … out … in … again and again." (Man, 65, lung cancer)

Yet, as this same patient described later in the interview, such a moment can once again give way to the fear of what is to come. This same man also said that he had learned a way to quiet his mind so that he was able to return to the here and now. This pointed to the reality that coping with a life-threatening disease involved a psychological, strongly oscillating process, out of which a new balance could eventually arise.

The view of Reality and the experience of Self during the treatments

At this stage, patients could get stuck in their process or were able to move to a place where they could begin to grieve. This mourning was a crucial moment in dealing with their predicament and a number of characteristics came to the fore.

- *mourning: letting go and making room for new meaning*

The process of mourning always involves finding the courage to let go of familiar frameworks of meaning, of a trusted and stable identity. The courage to do this is not immediately at the patient's disposal. Some of the patients we interviewed said that at such a moment they had the feeling of sinking into a bottomless pit or seeing themselves as sitting all alone, bereft, in the middle of a desert. Sometimes it was as if they were going through 'a dark night'. This is the existential crisis, which was outlined in Chapter One. In that chapter, we mentioned that we would return to this same topic in the third phase, which is where we are now.

There are different ways of dealing with an existential crisis, of being in a dark night. There were patients who could not find a way out. They were stuck in their fear, despair, powerlessness and sadness. Others were able to find a way to endure and deal with their existential crisis. In talking with our patients, we understood how important it is to be able to 'let go' of the old and familiar and to find the courage to work with the many emotions which surface. In doing so, an inner space can gradually open out on to unexpected perspectives on the meaning of their life.

Daring to grieve breaks through the process of being swung back and forth between powerful emotions. It brings release from being stuck at the extreme end of polarised emotions. If mourning creates space for new meaning to emerge, then this meaning is not rationally constructed on the basis of familiar frameworks. It is not invented by the patients, but discovered and somehow 'received'. No matter how difficult and painful the process of grieving, it appears to be the crucial psychic link in coping with a life-threatening disease, where life itself is at stake and life-size contradictions need to be reconciled.

This awareness of new meaning often involves a completely new physical and sensory openness to the surrounding reality. The man who in the previous quote found support in his breathing when he was in utter distress, described how at a later moment he: "went outside again for the first time to take a walk. At a certain moment, I wondered: what do I see here? It was simply the contour of a tree, but it was so new to me! It was overwhelming to see this as something so totally new and to name it. It was incredible that I could say: It is a tree." (Man, 65 years old, lung cancer). This shows that this other 'view of Reality' is not about defining something from an intellectual or philosophical point of view, but involves a direct, physical and concrete sensory experience.

- *rediscovering meaning: from emptiness to fullness*

A strong sensory response can therefore be part of that unexpected 'experience of meaning', breaking through the earlier congealed system of meanings. Something as simple as a tree, seeing it as if for the first time, can bring with it a whole new dimension. At the same time, such a simple word as 'tree' makes it possible to contain and preserve that unusual experience in the consciousness, giving it meaning and value.

This openness to such sensory experiences seems to thrive particularly in a more 'passive-receptive state of mind'. From the quotation cited above, it seems that such an experience of meaning is striking, sometimes even 'overwhelming'. It offers a whole new perspective on Reality that previously seemed so familiar. To use an expression from the philosopher Michel de Certeau, it signifies a *rupture in the pattern of meanings,* a breakthrough in that pattern that makes a renewal of meanings possible, encompassing even the physical senses.[11]

Experiencing Reality in a different way often goes hand in hand with a changed experience of the Self. The body also plays a decisive role here, as evidenced by what a woman said after having taken part in one of the psycho-energetic exercises:

"Once, while meditating, I had the experience of just being here and suddenly I was simply able to just lie here without all those disturbing thoughts about whether I was doing this the right way. At that moment, I felt a deep connection with everything. I was completely in the present moment and at the same time I also had the experience of being nowhere!" (Woman, 53 years old, breast cancer)

A curious paradoxical experience emerges in this last statement. Instead of Hamlet's 'to be **or** not to be', this signifies a 'to be **and** not to be'. Living with paradox is a core element of a lived and embodied spirituality.

- *connectedness and autonomy*

Patients who find the courage to let go of many things that are so familiar and safe, experience something in which a deep connection with 'a greater whole' can be heard. This can be regarded as a natural and deeply felt experience of meaning. It often coincides with a moment of psychological and physical relaxation, which appears to induce greater sensitivity and openness towards such an experience. A physical and mental state of relaxation paves the way for deeper contact with the body, making it possible to experience a fuller sense and meaning of Reality.

This sense of connectedness can be experienced by people in their personal-social environment, with the whole of humanity and wider creation: "Suddenly

---

[11] de Certeau, M. (1966) 'Culture and spiritual experience', *Concilium* 19, no.1, 3–31.

I heard the beating of my heart and I thought: this is a part of nature here within me. And then I felt that I myself was part of nature ..." (woman, 53 years old, breast cancer)

For some, it can also mean a sense of connectedness with a transcendent dimension, such as 'the Infinite' or God.

It is striking that this connection with a greater whole also points to a new experience of the Self. The woman quoted above who felt a deep connection with everything, also said: "I am now more myself than ever before." (Woman, 53 years old, breast cancer)

This woman also spoke about being less dependent on the expectations of others. Here, the paradoxical aspect meant that 'being more herself' went hand in hand with a more open and tolerant attitude towards those around her: "I was no longer so demanding towards my husband. I used to ask for his unceasing support. Letting go of these demands was a relief for both of us."

This new quality of relating to others largely dissolves the feeling of deep loneliness that is often so prevalent in 'the dark night' of an existential crisis. Feeling connected with a greater whole, whilst simultaneously preserving personal autonomy, is therefore another element of a lived and embodied spirituality.

What we learned from this third stage

We found that patients are really 'forced' into their bodies when having medical treatments that are often very difficult to endure. It is during these times that they feel intensely miserable, often unable to ignore the reality that they exist in a body. It is in physical suffering that the body makes itself present in an unmistakable and inescapable way, and this must be accepted.

As a result of their intense physical suffering, patients increasingly perceive themselves as a 'subject' in their body, which counteracts the experience of being an 'object' of medical treatment. As a consequence, they often express themselves more personally and directly, without feeling the need to hold back for the sake of complying with what others expect of them. The experience of being just a number within an impersonal standardised medical system can actually lead to patients becoming more articulate, sometimes even rebellious.

We discovered that deeper contact with the body can help to anchor the panicky mind in 'the here and now', stopping the obsessive thinking about a threatening future. Really experiencing the body as it is in the moment creates a space in which unexpected meanings can surface. These moments, which seem to come 'as gift', carry a patient beyond the pain and misery to a place where life can be experienced in the present moment, in all its fullness.

Grieving what has been lost is an important process of transition. It allows for an inner space to be carved out in which a patient becomes more receptive to new meanings.

We have already said that coping with a life-threatening disease involves an oscillating process, struggling with the hard facts of life and death. It involves learning to tolerate extreme psychological opposites, reconciling them and allowing space for them in a broader context. Finding a balance between these opposites at a more encompassing level hints at the *dialectical nature* of this process.

At this stage of the disease process, the set and fixed view of reality and identity begins to change. These changes are initiated by the changing experience of the body. This points to the reality that a person's new sense of reality and identity are not just cognitive, rational learning processes, but rooted in the body, making it a core aspect of an embodied spirituality.

Stage 4: The 'reconciled body'

hoc est enim corpus meum (this is indeed my body)

The experience of the body five years after treatment

This is the stage when the disease and the treatments are somewhere in the past and normal life has started to return. Yet many patients said that life after cancer would never again be taken for granted, as it was before their illness. At this stage, patients often experience a new relationship with their bodies.

- *healed, yet still with a disquieting source of uncertainty*

It was clear that the careless, naive attitude which patients had towards their bodies before they became ill had now disappeared for ever. Medical check-ups, for example, are often accompanied with a fear that something could be wrong again. What were once regarded as minor and innocent complaints, such as a cold, a little bump or a cough, become a disquieting cause of suspicion.

The physical, psychological and social after-effects of a disease such as cancer often have major consequences for aspects of life such as work, insurance options, negotiating mortgages and so on. After-effects in the experience of the body can also persist for a long time in the relationship with the partner, sexuality, fertility and the overall sense of self-esteem.

- *finally reconciled with its limitations*

We wrote earlier that dealing with illness and coping with an existential crisis may trigger an intense process of mourning. This can also happen during the stage when people have recovered enough to resume normal life and suddenly find themselves confronted with boundaries that were not there before. This is the time when physical, psychological and energetic limitations need to be acknowledged and taken into account.

The fulfilment of some desires may no longer be possible and the limits to what is possible need to be faced. The gap between desires and limitations opens up. Finding a balance between what is desired and what is possible in reality requires courage. It means searching for the creativity and practical wisdom that lies hidden within the person: "I used to want to change the whole world. These days I can't aim for that anymore. It is meaningless and just wastes energy. I only do what I can do. That's all." (woman, 53, breast cancer)

Becoming reconciled with the body, with its limitations, is an important step to becoming reconciled with life as it is. The important, leading role the body plays in this can be heard in the sigh: "Yes, this is simply my body!" (In Catholic liturgy: "hoc est enim corpus meum!")

The view of Reality and the experience of Self, five years after treatment

It is often the case that after five years following treatment, patients view themselves and their place in the world in a new way. Their views on the reality of life and death and their sense of who they are as a person are significantly changed.

- *widening the framework of meaning*

Among a number of the patients we interviewed, the process of becoming reconciled with the body was an important step towards gaining a new perspective on life. Life turns out to be different to how it was and how they hoped it would be. Vulnerability, finiteness and mortality need to be given a place.

It is not only the disruptive experience of a life-threatening illness that needs to be given a place, but also those strange experiences of being absorbed into a larger whole, together with the unexpected peace of mind that comes with this. These unusual and rather paradoxical experiences appear to bring great comfort and provide a way of making peace with life, as it is, in the present moment. This reconfigured way of looking at the world means that what might initially seem strange, incomprehensible, 'vague' or even 'crazy' is given a place.

- *widening the space for who I really am*

Two apparently opposing psychic dispositions need to be integrated: a receptive disposition to being open to experiences of meaning and a more active psychological disposition where such experiences are taken seriously. The balance between a passive and an active disposition leads to a broadening and restructuring of the Self, to new ways of being and acting in the world.

Conscious of the fact that life is transient, many (ex) patients become much more open to the 'blessings of the moment', more consciously aware of them. They grow in their understanding of what is important:

"If I am in touch with my own energy, my insight into things is very accurate and my feelings about things are correct. It's at such a moment that I know exactly what is good and not good for me. I know what I need. And that does not have to agree with what others around me need. It is about my need at that particular moment." (Woman, 63 years old, breast cancer)

This new psychic 'robustness' gives patients' room to be more themselves and less dependent on others. It marks a fundamental change in the basic sense of life. Patients accept who they really are deep down, which is something unprecedented for them: "That I can finally allow myself to be the way I am … From the moment I could let go of the idea of how I should be … and how the church had told us (my mother and me) how we had to be, I was in touch again with a sense of joy in my life." (Woman, 52 years old, colon cancer)

This growth in self-confidence brings with it a more expansive space for allowing and naming emotions ... including the 'negative' ones ... and therefore for experiencing life itself with all its ups and downs:

"And what this brings is much more love towards myself ... I can be very happy when I realise that everything exists side by side and that, in the end, everything changes. In a moment when I feel very sad, I say to myself: okay, just let it be and I allow myself to stay with that feeling. And the next moment I am washing the dishes and find myself thinking how wonderful life is. I have everything. Emotions change from one moment to the next and knowing and accepting this gives me confidence." (Woman, 53 years old, breast cancer)

What we learned from this fourth stage

In our patients, the experience of becoming reconciled with the body involves a process of becoming more reconciled with life and death. It is at this stage of the disease process that patients no longer experience themselves as completely alienated from their bodies. The body, which in the hospital was often experienced as an object of medical-technical treatment, has been re-appropriated. The patients we interviewed showed what a profound and often surprising process this was.

It is clear that also in this fourth stage, the experience of the body again plays a crucial role. Both the acceptance of the physical limitations and the experience of 'being part of a larger whole' happen in and through the body. This is not simply a philosophical idea or a form of wishful thinking, but a physically experienced reality.

The way in which patients talk about this means that this is not created artificially or evoked in the imagination, but often comes unexpectedly and spontaneously from within. Deep relaxation during some of the meditative, psycho-energetic exercises can create a condition that elicits and supports this experience.

Remarkably, a number of patients said that the fear of death was absent in this experience. There is a 'fullness of life', a sense of fulfilment which brings joy and a deep knowing that this is not divorced from earthly reality. This embodied spirituality involves: going into 'the dark night', losing meaning and identity, mourning the losses, letting go of illusions and … discovering new meanings.

In this context, 'spirituality' is not about extraordinary experiences of being absorbed within the infinity of a greater whole and living in perpetual bliss. Fixing it down in this way would simply mean that it was pointing to something static. It is in fact a dynamic process in which people learn to live with paradox.

A lived and embodied spirituality:

- Radically breaks through the separation between body and mind. It is through physical suffering that people are 'drawn' into the reality of their body, so that it no longer can be ignored;
- involves the struggle between what can often be perceived as irreconcilable realities of life and death, where people are hurled back and forth between opposite poles;
- entails a dialectical process, in which people learn to reconcile and integrate contradictory and paradoxical realities at a deeper level;
- triggers a process of mourning during which illusions about the invulnerability of the body and the idea that life never ends have to be given up;
- involves having to let go of illusory ideas about the self, so that the reality of the naked 'me' can emerge: 'losing me, to become me';
- manifests itself in a life which is lived between a sense of limitedness and of limitlessness, a sense of feeling trapped within life's boundaries, yet of being part of a larger whole;
- shows itself in a life which is lived between a receptive and an active disposition towards life,
- Recognises that our search for meaning and the acceptance of reality is rooted in the body.

Embodied spirituality entails a process of 'Losing me, Becoming me'— hence the title of this book.

Chapter Three
The Body as an Instrument,
The Body as a Space of Experience

Shifts and changes: Is there a pattern?

From listening to our patients, it became clear that they often talked about radical shifts and changes in the way they experienced their body during the different stages of their illness. We highlighted the relationship of these changes with changes in the patients' perspective of Reality and experience of the Self. We will now look at the diverse experiences of our patients from within two categories that emerged when we listened to them speaking about the changing experiences of their body.

These categories helped us to look beneath the surface of what patients experienced in and through their body. We named these categories: *functional-instrumental* and *sensory-sensitive* experiences. By using these categories, we were able to identify specific patterns of bodily awareness in each of the aforementioned four stages, namely:

- life before the illness;
- the moment of diagnosis;
- the period during medical treatment;
- and five years after their treatment.

There is a pattern to each stage. By putting the patterns together, we were able to discover an overarching pattern, an evolving story, with all the shifts and changes that are part of struggling with a life-threatening disease. This also provides a foundation for an embodied spirituality, a vision of spirituality as a process that is grounded in the body.

The functional-instrumental and sensory-sensitive experiences of the body

The *functional-instrumental* (FI) mode of experiencing the body refers to the body as the instrument through which people realise their goals in the future and the world outside. This mode of being describes how a person experiences him/herself as an active and autonomous functioning individual. This mode of experiencing the body manifests itself primarily in 'doing'.

The *sensory-sensitive* (SS) mode of experiencing the body refers to the manner in which the body is perceived and sensed through a range of both pleasant and unpleasant sensations. These are always experienced in the 'here and now' and occur within the space of the body. It is a state of 'being' rather than 'doing'. This mode of being means that the individual senses the world in an open, passive-receptive way.

The distinction between these two modes of 'doing' and 'being' can also be stated as 'the body that you have and use' (FI), compared to 'the body that you are and experience' (SS).

We now describe the specific pattern in each of the four stages.

Stage 1: The experience of the body before illness sets in

Reading and analysing the interviews, we discovered that before illness sets in, the functional-instrumental mode of being is dominant (FI +). People are mainly focused on achieving goals which lie in the outside world and are directed to the future. As an autonomous subject of their actions, people experience themselves as being active and in control of their lives.

Before people become ill, the sensory-sensitive (SS) mode of being, in which the body is experienced in a sensuous-pleasurable way, is clearly subordinate to the FI mode. This SS mode of being serves the body's need to rest and recuperate from work and, therefore, regain the energy needed to be active again in the world outside.

We visualised these two modes in a matrix in which the dominance of the functional-instrumental mode compared to the sensory-sensitive mode is shown by a dot in the upper right-hand square (quadrant).

SS FI	Sensory-sensitive +	Sensory-sensitive -
Functional-instrumental +	stage 4	stage 1 •
Functional-instrumental -	stage 3	stage 2

Stage 2: The patients' experience of the body during and after diagnosis

During or shortly after diagnosis, the autonomous and active way of being (the FI mode) becomes paralysed. It frequently happens that people feel emotionally and physically 'clapped-out', utterly undone. This means that neither the functional-instrumental nor the sensory-sensitive modes of experiencing the body are apparent. Neither is dominant. This situation is represented by a dot in the lower right-hand square of the matrix.

SS FI	Sensory-sensitive +	Sensory-sensitive -
Functional-instrumental +	stage 4	stage 1
Functional-instrumental -	stage 3	stage 2 •

Stage 3: The patients' experience of the body during treatment

In nearly all the patients during the phase of medical treatment, the negative experience of the body increases markedly. This means that the sensory-sensitive mode comes very much to the fore. The feeling of being a victim, perceiving oneself as a powerless object in relation to the illness, the side effects of the treatment and the prescribed medical procedures are very much present during this stage. Bodily suffering becomes so intense that all the attention is focused on the body, in the here and now.

In contrast to the first stage, the sensory-sensitive mode of experiencing the body is now dominant (SS +) with the functional-instrumental mode being subordinate (FI -). In this stage, the patient is no longer able to focus on attaining future goals and of being active in the outside world.

However, despite all the physical and emotional misery, unusual and unexpected experiences of meaning also occur at a very physical and sensory level. These are a manifestation of the sensory-sensitive mode which makes itself felt in a completely different way than in suffering and misery.

48

The sensory-sensitive mode which is dominant in this stage is represented by a dot in the lower left-hand quadrant of our matrix.

	Sensory-sensitive +	Sensory-sensitive -
Functional-instrumental +	stage 4	stage 1
Functional-instrumental -	stage 3 •	stage 2

Stage 4: The patients' experience of the body after treatment

The pattern which emerges after treatment is based on the experiences of the two groups of patients[12] who had completed their medical treatment five years previously. During the time after treatment the physical discomforts usually lessen and people start to feel better again. Virtually, all the patients who had ended their treatment some time before being interviewed said that they were once again experiencing positive feelings and felt more at home in their bodies.

It is, of course, important to realise that these patients do not represent all patients with cancer. They are the 'survivors'. Despite a number of limitations, they are able to be more active and expand their range of activities and imagine goals for the future. It is during this phase that the functional-instrumental mode of experiencing the body once again comes to the fore, but in a different way. Most people begin to find a new balance between the functional-instrumental and the sensory-sensitive modes of being. This is represented with a dot in the upper left-hand square of the matrix.

SS FI	Sensory-sensitive +	Sensory-sensitive -
Functional-instrumental +	stage 4 •	stage 1
Functional-instrumental -	stage 3	stage 2

The basic process of the patients' changing experience of the body in the four stages

---

[12] Description of the three groups of patients we interviewed, as described in the footnote in Chapter One.

The two categories used to describe the experience of the body during the various stages of the disease give a clear indication of the major changes to how the body is experienced during the four stages. In the matrix shown below, the shift in the relationship between the functional-instrumental and sensory-sensitive modes of being is shown by the arrows that lead from one stage of the disease process to the other and from one mode of experiencing the body to the other. In this way, they show the basic pattern as a movement of the changes which are experienced in the body.

SS FI	Sensory-sensitive +	Sensory-sensitive -
Functional-instrumental +	stage 4 •	stage 1 • ↓
Functional-instrumental -	↑ stage 3 •	← stage 2 •

It is remarkable that when we compare the two groups of patients who had completed their medical treatment five years earlier, then the patients in both of these groups seem to have achieved a balance between the functional-instrumental and sensory-sensitive modes of being. Although one group had received psycho-social counselling and the other had not, some kind of balance between these two categories exists in both groups. It seems that participating in psycho-social counselling makes no difference.[13]

Apparently the formulation of the two modes of bodily awareness is sufficiently abstract and encompassing that the experiences of all patients can be captured and understood. On the other hand, these two modes are abstract to such an extent that the differences between these groups—which are definitely there—do not become visible.

Nevertheless, these differences are striking and will be described extensively in the next chapter. To uncover the often remarkable differences in the three groups of patients, an additional way of analysing and interpreting the words of the patients is necessary. This will also be described in the next chapter.

---

[13] Of course, there are exceptions to the rule. It happens more than once that a patient gets stuck in one of the stages described above. In that case, psycho-social counselling or even psychotherapeutic treatment is needed to help someone to get out of this state of stagnation and discover a freedom of living which enables the two apparently contradictory poles to be embraced.

Conclusions regarding 'embodied spirituality'
Suffering: unravelling the separation between body and mind

At the moment, when cancer is diagnosed (stage 2) and during the period of medical treatment (stage 3), the experience of a deep and often painful separation between body and mind manifests itself very powerfully. A patient with a potentially fatal disease can feel strongly alienated from the body, even standing in opposition to it. The idea of being treated as an object within medical-technical practices reinforces this. And yet, the physical suffering which the patient has to endure makes it impossible to maintain that distance; the suffering 'sucks' him into his/her own body. Because of the suffering, the separation between the body and mind begins to unravel.

Suffering, an intense sensory-sensitive mode of experiencing the body, can be seen as a pivotal moment for engaging more deeply with the reality of the body. We have also seen that it is not only in suffering but also in some unusual and sometimes blissful experiences of perceiving oneself as part of a greater whole that the sensory-sensitive mode manifests itself. This mode of being counteracts the functional-instrumental mode, which is often extremely dominant when people are fit and healthy.

This deeper sensory-sensitive experience of the body, which involves a physical connectedness with Reality-as-it-is, is an essential aspect of an embodied spirituality.

Reconciliation: balancing two contradictory poles

In the previous chapter, we wrote about how coping with a life-threatening disease involves a process that is often marked by a fiercely oscillating character, played out between two poles. Sometimes a patient can get stuck in one of these poles, staying hopeless and helpless or resisting and denying the reality of what is going on.

Ideally, this process eventually resolves itself into a 'dialectical' movement, in which contradictions become reconciled and people learn to find a balance between these poles. It is in the fourth stage of the disease process that patients seem to find a balance between these two FI and SS modes and discover how to live again or perhaps for the first time in their lives, with the inherently paradoxical nature of their human existence.

'Embodied spirituality' means learning to live between the two modes of experiencing the body. In other words: living in the midst of doing and being. Time and again, and often changing in the course of one day, a paradoxical balance needs to be found.

Today, the word 'spirituality' can too often conjure up images of the desire to find life-long bliss, free of the nitty-gritty of ordinary life. But this is not what we mean when we speak of an 'embodied spirituality'. What we are describing is a way of being and acting in the world which involves facing and embracing 'Reality-as-it-is'.

It also means accepting the actual experience of our bodies, whilst at the same time integrating and giving voice to this. An active and receptive disposition towards life is needed for this to happen. Encompassing what appear to be contradictory attitudes allows life, with all its paradoxes, to be lived to the full.

The Self that we are is always more than we can ever put into words. This is also true for Reality-as-it-is, in its depth and vastness. It is this paradoxical way of living life which will come to the fore in the following chapters.

Chapter Four
Moments of Transition and Experience
of Transcendence

Remarkable differences between the three groups of patients

Despite the great similarity in the basic pattern of how changes in the body were experienced by the patients within the three groups,[14] clear differences could also be observed. Among those patients for whom the period of sickness, with all its treatments, had ended five years before (groups 1 and 3), certain differences started to emerge in the third stage (the treatment stage), but became increasingly clear in the fourth stage.

A first difference between both groups emerged when patients from the group which had no counselling (group 3) spoke more than once about 'feeling like their old selves' again, whilst the group which received counselling (group 1) spoke nearly always about feeling quite different now as a person. They spoke about having strangely new experiences, which even seemed to have a transcendent quality to them.

As stated in the first chapter, the aim of our research was to gain deeper insight into the connection between the changes in the way the body was experienced and aspects of spirituality which come to light as a result of this. By exploring this connection among people, who, because of their sickness, are unable to ignore their bodily reality, the concept of spirituality becomes more physically grounded.

It is not surprising that the patients in groups 1 and 2 were more explicit about the particular and striking changes in the way they perceived their body. Restoring and deepening the contact with the body formed an essential part of

---

[14] Description of the three groups of patients we interviewed, as described in the footnote in Chapter One.

the support and counselling provided at Tabor House. In fact, the psycho-energetic bodywork within this programme involved a systematic exploration and deepening of the sensory-sensitive experience of the body. The sometimes unusual experiences in the way the body was perceived often resulted in interesting perspectives on ancient themes around mind and body and spirituality and corporeality. Patients often described this relationship in new, more nuanced and sometimes surprising ways.

Back to the old self or never again the old self!
Group 3: back to the old self?

Ex-patients from group 3 who did not have any form of counselling during their illness often said that, after some time, they once again felt like their 'old self'. Once their treatment was over, a number of these ex-patients said that they were able to pick up the thread of their life as it had been before their illness. A man of 67, who had colon cancer, said: "I was operated on; it was not a big deal and you simply got on with life. I still believe that I will reach the age of 100, just like my mother when she died." A woman from this group said that after her operation—despite some serious physical restrictions and having to let go of many things—she was still the same person she had been before she became ill: "I've always been a very intense person and still am, but in a different way." (Woman, 58 years old, lung cancer)

The perception of these patients was that they were once more like their 'old selves'. 'Becoming the old self' is, of course, a relative concept because a number of changes, such as an amputation and loss of energy, are actually irreversible and will impact on the rest of their lives. Patients in this group also often spoke in a positive way about having learned from their period of sickness, about living more in the here and now, being more respectful towards themselves and others and often about having a deeper relationship with their partner. Even so, they still frequently spoke about the return of the 'old me'.

Recovering the 'old life', which this group of patients spoke about, can be attributed to the fact that all of them were still alive five years after being diagnosed with cancer and, with one exception, all had a favourable prognosis. This could also be the reason why none of them experienced an existential crisis and were spared the journey through the 'dark night of the soul'. The one exception to this was the patient who had received an unfavourable prognosis and had exclaimed: "Lung cancer, dead little birdie!"

Groups 1 and 2: never again the old self!

The patients in groups 1 and 2 who came for counselling at Tabor House tended to have an unfavourable or at least a very uncertain prognosis. Many of them had experienced an existential crisis. Their struggle with this was one of the reasons why they asked for psycho-social support. When asked how they felt five years after their treatment, they talked about feeling profoundly changed in the way they experienced the body, themselves and their connection with life. This was especially true for patients from group one. They expressed this as being more:

- in contact with the body;
- in contact with the centre of the body and therefore more in contact with themselves;
- deeply connected with and within 'a larger whole'.

Moments of transition: incarnation, centring, transcendence:

The repeated use of terms like 'more' and 'deeper' was striking. They point to experiences which are perceived as moments when patients cross some boundary. We formulated these events as *moments of transition.* We identified and described them using three concepts which point to key movements: **incarnation, centring and transcendence.**

'**Incarnation**' describes the movement in which patients experience themselves as becoming more aware of their body, learning to accept it as it is, becoming more deeply connected with it.

'**Centring**' means becoming more deeply in contact with the centre of the body. This seems to go together with the experience of a stronger contact with the self. There is often a physical, psychological and even spiritual dimension to becoming more centred within the body.

'**Transcendence**' is about an increasing sense of being part of a larger whole. It also refers to the more common meaning of this word, which indicates the transition into a more spacious, deeper, higher dimension of reality.

These three processes provide useful links to the way in which patients of groups 1 and 2 approached their disease. The words *incarnation* and *transcendence* point to rich and highly charged meanings, especially in theology and spirituality. In these fields, they touch on the corporeal, psychological, theological and spiritual aspects of existence.

Whilst the concepts of incarnation and transcendence are very common within the language of spirituality and theology, the concept of *centring*, where a person discovers a psycho-spiritual centre lying in the very midst of the body, is much less common. In this and the following chapters, it will become clear that the term centring is an essential addition to the other two. It forms the mediating, integrating factor between the seemingly opposite poles of incarnation and transcendence. It points to the dialectical process which we described in Chapter Three. Centring is a process which helps to give focus and direction when patients are struggling with huge and paradoxical contradictions in feelings and thoughts.

The functional-instrumental and sensory-sensitive experience of the body which we explored in Chapter Three will now be described using the concepts incarnation, centring and transcendence as a process. Using these terms offers the possibility of gaining deeper insight into some of the unusual ways in which the patients of groups 1 and 2 related to their body. Their experiences of *moments of transition* were remarkedly different from the way in which patients in group 3 talked about their body. These transitional experiences of the patients of groups 1 and 2 shed a special light on essential aspects of embodied spirituality.

The differences between the groups
A comparison based on 'moments of transition'

When we compared the groups of patients, the first thing we noticed was the different ways in which those in groups 1 and 3 described their sensory-sensitive bodily awareness. This had already come to the fore during the treatment stage, but was strongly present during life after treatment.

In group 3, which was made up of patients who had received no counselling at Tabor House and who did not do any psycho-energetic bodywork, the moments of transition only occurred to a limited degree. Moreover, there seems to be hardly any coherence apparent between a deeper contact with the body (incarnation), with oneself (centring) and with a larger whole (transcendence).

In group 1, which was made up of patients who had counselling and participated in psycho-energetic bodywork, there was considerably more variation in what can be described as 'moments of transition', whereby all the patients experienced such moments. The cohesion between the three areas of incarnation, centring and transcendence was striking and meant that patients described a feeling of wholeness.

In group 2, which was made up of patients that were still undergoing medical treatment and had taken part in a basic programme of psycho-energetic bodywork, statements about one or more of the three areas were frequently made. These were less frequent than in group 1, but significantly more than in group 3. The cohesion between the different categories was also less present than in group 1, but more so than in group 3. This was quite remarkable for a group which was still having medical treatment and had not yet been able to find a balance between the functional-instrumental and the sensory-sensitive ways of experiencing the body.

It is not surprising that the patients we interviewed in groups 1 and 2 were able to describe themselves as being more in contact with their body and its centre. It would have been strange if such experiences had not been reported. However, what did surprise us was the way that, in wholly unexpected ways, patients experienced themselves as part of a greater whole. Patients hesitantly searched for words to describe their very individual and authentic experiences. These were not 'moments of transition', but 'experiences of transcendence' which somehow more clearly defined the difference between groups 1 and 3.

Experiences of transcendence

The experiences of transcendence were of a different order to those moments of transition described above. Indeed, they were not perceived as fleeting and short-lived but stayed with the patients for a long time. Such moments carried within them the potential for looking at Reality and perceiving the Self in a different way. When speaking about these moments of transcendence, patients described another dimension, something they had never previously known. They emphasised the special character and the reality which such experiences held for them: "Sometimes my eyes are closed and then it is … yes, indeed, it is very odd, I don't know how to say it … it is as if the sun breaks through. It is something that happens within me. It is a light that cannot really be described in the way that we often speak of light." (Woman, 57 years, breast cancer)

We were able to see just how unique and personal these experiences were by noticing how tentatively patients spoke about them. Whilst the moments of transition, such as having more contact with the body and its centre, were a fixed part of the psycho-energetic bodywork, the content of experiences of transcendence had a completely original and authentic ring to them. For the patient, they involved an individual experience and emotional quality, often being described through words such as 'space', 'energy' and 'light'.

Experiences of transcendence: space, energy and light

Space

When taking part in the psycho-energetic work with the body, a number of patients had a strong experience of an inner 'space'. This way of working with the body invites participants to turn their focus inwards. 'Turning inwards' means discovering a breathing space within the centre of the body. One of the patients said: "The exercises … help me to turn inwards, to get out of my head. They bring me into contact with a place within myself where I am less busy with thinking; a space where there is only breathing. When I focus on my breathing in this way, I perceive space and yes … light and yes … emptiness and silence …" (woman, 57, breast cancer, kidney cancer)

This innermost breathing space also creates a space which extends from deep within to a space outside the self. The contours of the body's skin are no longer perceived as a closed-off boundary, but a permeable border that is open to the space surrounding the body: "The contours of my body fade, it becomes more than just my material body." It is from out of this sensation of dissolving boundaries that the boundary of the body is perceived at the end of a meditation, in an unusual and remarkably new way. "I surely know that sensation of spaciousness which I experience during such a meditative exercise. When I open my eyes after such an experience, I have the feeling of having to find my way back into the contours of this skin. That space is smaller, more limited than where I was before, than the spaciousness I had just experienced." (Woman, 57, breast cancer, kidney cancer)

Another patient gave a religious interpretation of the experience of space, even though she spoke about an absence of any religious upbringing at home: "To be connected to that infinite space … of tranquillity, peace, light, of harmony … For me, this is the ultimate reality which I would now call God." (Woman, 54, breast cancer)

For this patient, this experience of spaciousness seems to have a paradoxical quality about it. The space is clearly perceived as something which can be found deep within her and at the same time as something surrounding her. She describes it in the following way: "I sometimes think that this space is within myself, but at the same time that I am also in it … God is in me, but I am also in God! … It is bigger than I am. It also encompasses you and other people; it includes us all. At the same time, there is also a connection, as it were, with ourselves, with a place within ourselves. Sometimes it is very close to us, it is within us."

This feeling of being absorbed within a great spaciousness, whilst at the same time remaining very close to the self, was also experienced by a man as he walked along the beach: "Whilst walking there I could see an expanse of space surrounding me. Although I find it hard to describe the physicality of this experience, it was as if heaven opened up and I found myself standing within that space. I felt so deeply connected to it, as if I was really in it. Even though it is difficult to understand this, it was as if I was projecting something out into that space, which is actually here within myself. It involved a really powerful interaction … But I did not lose myself in it. I stood there … I realised that I was there. The space surrounded me and was within me … It touched the very depths of me. It went so deep. This is why I call it a sacred space." (Man, 65, lung cancer)

Reflection: experiencing space and embodied spirituality

Over and over again, a number of elements seem to occur in these perceptions of space. The first step to experiencing such a space involves 'going within', going inside yourself. This is not primarily about arriving at the place of deep feeling or deep thought, but of experiencing breath in the depths of the abdomen and the pelvis. This focus on the 'breathing centre' induces a deep sense of relaxation that permeates the whole body, something which even extends to the skin around the body. For some, it seems as if the skin itself dissolves and they feel absorbed into a larger space. The skin is experienced as an organ which breathes with them, which of course it does, though it is rarely experienced in this way. It is also remarkable that despite the fact that patients felt they were being absorbed within an infinite space, they still felt very much in contact with themselves.

Making contact with the body as a whole and with its centre formed a standard part of the psycho-energetic bodywork that was offered at Tabor House. The descriptions of transcendence are entirely personal and authentic. It is important to stress that when experiences are purposely induced in the patients by the therapist, then this flies in the face of the principles which underpin psycho-energetic bodywork. Inducing this kind of experience would constitute a form of hypnosis. This is not what psycho-energetic bodywork is about.

Our interviews with patients bring to light dimensions of transcendence, which were unknown to us and were described by patients in a very personal and unique way. The discovery of an inner and outer space opened up a special dimension in the sensory-sensitive way of experiencing the body, which deepened our perspective on an embodied spirituality.

Energy

Another experience of transcendence that occurred through the psycho-energetic bodywork was that of a powerful 'flow of energy' through the body. This adds another dimension to the way the body is usually experienced and creates a deeper, sensory-sensitive aspect to this: "What I could very much sense was that there is also something like a flow of energy which can bring about a remarkable change in your body." (Woman, 54, breast cancer)

For this woman, this different experience was not something that remained restricted to her body but unfolded into another way of seeing Reality: "It is through the psycho-energetic body work that I experience something which is also imperishable within me … an invisible, not so tangible, but still perceptible world … This brings another dimension to my life that was not there before, a spiritual dimension."

The experience that this flowing energy brings with it points to another dimension of bodily awareness which is described by this woman as 'the soul body', a reality that is physical, but not in the concrete and material sense, as she previously understood it: "The energy flows are within me and … in the soul body, so it is even more intangible! This truly is an extra dimension in my life."

The experience of this flowing energy is not something that only occurs inside the body. The man we quoted earlier also noticed that he experienced a strong exchange between the energy which entered him from the outside and then went out again from within. Experiencing energy in this way is not just an introverted, intrapsychic event. It seems to be based on a strong sense of interaction between an inner and outer world: "Yes, there is also a real physical sensation to it. It tingles through my body, it flows. The energy enters and leaves me from every side, creating a sense of warmth throughout my body." (Man, 65 years old, lung cancer). This streaming energy is not something abstract, but it is something experienced within the body as being concrete: as a tingling feeling, a warmth which moves through the body.

It goes without saying that not every patient is sensitive to this flow of energy. A woman told us that she did not have the experiences that others sometimes talked about. She attributed this to her tendency of doing the exercises very much from her head and with too much effort. It was through the experience of a massage at Tabor House [5] that, much to her surprise, she was able to experience this flow of energy: "I really enjoyed those massages. The therapist touches you and everything starts to flow. It is very special. It leads to a real physical sensation of flowing energy. How is that possible? I tend to be one of those people who does not feel anything and often does not know what it is that I am supposed to feel, but this was very real! It was extremely physical and pleasant." (Woman, 55 years, Kahler's disease and breast cancer)

Reflection: experiencing energy and embodied spirituality

Experiencing energy in this way gives an extra dimension to perceiving the body in a sensory-sensitive way. Whilst 'energy' appears to be a fairly abstract concept, patients perceive it in a very physical manner, describing experiences of currents of energy, tingling and warmth passing through the body. It brings with it a completely different experience to the way in which each person perceives their body. One of the patients talked about experiencing a 'soul body' which represents a different, 'imperishable' dimension within the reality of her life: something that was invisible and not tangible.

---

[15] This specifically refers to haptonomic massage which was offered at Tabor House, Nijmegen.

This experience of flowing energy within the body is also perceived as a bridge linking the inner and outer world. The energy experienced within the body seems to come from the outside but also flows from inside-out. This interaction is perhaps a very energetic explanation of the feeling that patients often speak about, namely that of 'being absorbed into a larger whole', something which, as we saw in Chapter One, seems to lie at the very essence of the experience of meaning. In Chapter Two, we saw that experiencing the self in this way was an important aspect of embodied spirituality.

In Chapters Six and Seven, when we look in-depth at the traditions of Qi Gong and hesychasm, we will revisit this experience of energy flowing through the body and consider it from within a psycho-spiritual framework.

Light

Patients also speak about experiencing 'light', when they describe moments of transcendence. This clearly emerges in the account of the man who, whilst walking on the beach, experienced being in a sacred space filled with light, wherein he felt deeply connected: "I find it difficult to say what actually happened there. It was not something I saw with my eyes, but everything lit up. There was another light. There was a new glow … everything was lit up differently. Everything. Even the way I felt. Indeed, also the way I felt, perceived and experienced … I did not know anything about this sort of thing before, but I was perceiving something in a new way, perhaps with a different form of consciousness. If only it could always be like this, but it is not normal. Not for me, no…" (Man, 65 years old, lung cancer)

The experience of light can also mark those moments when something 'breaks' through the darkness of pain and suffering. This was expressed in the following way by a patient who at first saw her various points of pain and diseased areas in her body (head, chest, abdomen) as a dark and heavy cross which she was carrying in herself. During one of the psycho-energetic meditation exercises, the following happened: "That cross that I felt and experienced within me, it suddenly gave light, literally! I felt it and saw it. Flames and light were coming out of it. The cross became light, a shining cross. It was so special that it gave light … The heaviness of the black cross … suddenly became light and then it all changed. Also afterwards. Everything really changed. There was suddenly a light-giving cross." (Woman, 60 years old, breast cancer)

The woman who spoke earlier of a powerful experience of space ('an infinite space of peace, of light, of harmony') saw this as a light-filled space: "It happened once during a meditation exercise. I found myself looking into a huge space of light and had to open my eyes for a moment … It was as if the sun was suddenly shining brightly inside or … something like that. I wondered 'what is going on here'? But, the light of the room and the room itself … were actually no different." This was not a one and only experience for this woman, because "… I did have experiences of 'that light' during the meditations. I saw spaces around me which were full of light." This experience impacted profoundly on her: "… I realised I want to live for this, I want to die for this …" (woman, 54, breast cancer)

Reflection: experiencing light and embodied spirituality

The experience of light often appears to coincide with the experience of an inner space. It is as if this inner space manifests itself as light. The idea that light always has to come from the outside, like the light from the sun or a lamp, is challenged by this experience. As a transcendent experience, it 'lights up' from within. The patients who experienced these things led them to conclude that the light came from within—an inner light. It is this light coming from within themselves that illuminates everything around them. It also radiates through every aspect of themselves: their senses, feelings and consciousness. This experience of light can be regarded as an extraordinary sensory-sensitive experience in body, mind and soul.

This light also seems to be a force that can break through the darkness. With one of the patients, this was the darkness of suffering and pain experienced in various parts of her body. The cross of pain and physical suffering lit up and became 'lighter' to carry.

The transcendent experience of 'spaces of inner light' has great consequences and can be such an extraordinary moment that the woman quoted above said: "I want to live for this, I want to die for this."

This experience of inner light is definitely a remarkable aspect of embodied spirituality. It is also a crucial theme in the tradition of hesychasm where it is referred to as the light of Tabor. This will be described in more detail in Chapter Seven.

Embodied spirituality as the living paradox of transcendence and concrete physicality

A remarkable finding in the interviews was that these experiences of transcendence remained 'grounded' thanks to them being anchored in the experience of the body. Patients did not say that they were 'dissolving' into a larger whole, into a state beyond earthly reality, but talked about being clearly and concretely in touch with themselves and their body which could not be ignored because of the impact of the illness. This experience of transcendence and at the same time of being grounded within the concrete reality of body and life, seemed to hold together in a paradoxical balance. According to some patients, the whole struggle in coping with their illness and facing 'the Reality of life and death' was precisely about discovering and maintaining this balance. This balance was experienced as walking a 'middle' way between seemingly opposed realities, such as the reality of physical vulnerability and the transcendent experiences of energy, space and light described above. Both poles remained intact and were even more meaningful when understood within a broader context.

The following illustrates this balance between opposing realities: "I wouldn't describe it using the word 'dissolving'. It is an experience of becoming bigger than my body, yet my physical body remains as it is. If I dissolve, I disappear. But I actually become more present … Yes, I feel more encompassing … Truly, I am more present and it feels as if I am able to fill an entire space." (Woman, 57, breast cancer, kidney cancer)

Another patient also emphasised that she does not dissolve into 'the larger whole', but that she remains very concretely present in what she does, also in her role as a mother: "Yes, I am part of the whole, but I don't dissolve. I'm not nowhere anymore. I am here, I am part of the whole and now I am going to play the piano … then, at another moment, I am the mother of a daughter." (Woman, 63 years old, breast cancer, relapsed, unfavourable prognosis)

A final illustration is that of the woman we quoted earlier and who gives an explicit religious interpretation to the 'larger whole', but also emphasises that this does not mean that who she is as a person disappears. The paradoxical nature of her experience comes through clearly in what she says: "I sometimes think that this whole is within myself, but at the same time I am also within it … God is in me, but I am also in God! … And at the same time there is also a connection with ourselves, with a spot within ourselves. So sometimes it really is very close to us, within us." (Woman, 54 years old, breast cancer)

The above are three very clear illustrations of how opposites were being held together: the body as physical reality and the body as space; the immanent ('a spot in myself') and the transcendent ('God'); the concrete physical action ('playing the piano', 'being a mother') and the infinite ('experiencing a large whole').

This coming together of immanent and transcendent dimensions of Reality is a striking finding within this study. The separation that is often presupposed between these two dimensions of Reality does not seem to be present in the patients' experiences. The paradoxical connectedness of both dimensions points to a special aspect of lived and embodied spirituality.

Summary and conclusions

Embodied spirituality as a dialectical movement towards the 'middle'

We have seen that dealing with a life-threatening disease, as it unfolds during the different stages of the disease process, is a movement that initially can oscillate fiercely between strongly opposing realities, such as fight and surrender, hope and despair, fear and trust. It means living and enduring the full paradox of these moments of life. Ideally, this process gradually transforms into a more dialectical movement in which opposites find balance within a 'middle'. In discovering this balance, the essence of both poles is maintained and yet transformed into a state whereby conflicting opposites can complement each other.

It seems to become clear that the focus on finding the 'middle' gives direction to the process of embodied spirituality. This movement towards the middle acknowledges the paradoxical reality of 'living life in its fullness'. The polarities do not sacrifice anything at all of their reality, but instead they are transformed and transcended. This corrects the view of spirituality as a way of living which avoids the reality of life and aspires to the higher realms.

At the beginning of this chapter, we have formulated 'moments of transition' as *incarnation, centring* and *transcendence.* These terms help to anchor the process of lived spirituality within the body. This is something they have in common with the terms functional-instrumental and sensory-sensitive experiences of the body. But more than these latter two terms, the former constitute a trinity, something that points to the dialectical nature of embodied spirituality.

In the experience of a number of patients, centring was clearly connected with incarnation. It involves making connection with the body-as-it-is and especially with the centre of the body, in the space of the pelvis. At the same time, centring also connects directly with unusual experiences of transcendence, such as space, energy and light.

Centring, in the psycho-physical centre of the body, bridges the apparent contradiction between incarnation and transcendence. Going more deeply into the reality of the body's centre creates the condition for opening up the space beyond the body's boundaries. This is not only the space of the world around us—nature, life and the cosmos that encompasses us—but also of the divine, God. This means that centring is the connecting link between incarnation and transcendence and forms the basic dialectical dynamic in the process of a lived and embodied spirituality.

Part Two:
Three Perspectives of
Existential Phenomenology,
Qi Gong and Hesychasm

Chapter Five
Looking at Patients' Experiences Through Existential Phenomenology

We explored the concepts of incarnation, centring and transcendence in Chapter Four and presented them as essential aspects in a lived and embodied spirituality. We are now going to look more deeply into these concepts by considering them from within three very different philosophical and spiritual perspectives, namely: existential phenomenology as a recent Western philosophical movement; the physical-spiritual practices of Qi Gong within Chinese Daoism and hesychasm within Eastern Orthodox Christianity.

These three different perspectives are far apart in time and culture, but they each emphasise the importance of the body and bodily experience in psychological and spiritual growth. This also allows us to situate the patients' experiences within a wider perspective, which, in turn, can also be relevant to all human beings.

In this chapter, we will first look at existential phenomenology. As a recent philosophical movement, existential phenomenology is interesting because it is based on the reality of people in the Western world. It provides a sometimes unsettling analysis of the way that we in the West look at life, relate to death and experience our body. From the perspective of existential phenomenology, the concepts of *incarnation, centring* and *transcendence* have a very specific content. This makes it possible to understand the experiences of the patients at a deeper level.

Core ideas of existential phenomenology

Existential phenomenology is a philosophical movement which has its roots in the transition years of the nineteenth and twentieth century. It is a movement based primarily on the work of Edmund Husserl (1859–1938) and was developed further in the mid-twentieth century by philosophers such as Martin Heidegger, Maurice Merleau-Ponty and Jean-Paul Sartre.[16] Emmanuel Levinas and Jacques Derrida were also strongly influenced by existential phenomenology, but offered their own fundamental critique of it.

At the end of this chapter, we will focus on Levinas' critique, which is essential in order to do justice to particular aspects of the patients' experiences.

Within existential phenomenology, it is of utmost importance that a human being is not regarded as a disembodied consciousness, isolated from the world around him, as appears to be the case in René Descartes' philosophy.

On the contrary, through the very fibres of the body, a person is profoundly connected with the world around. When people think, feel and act they always do so in relationship to the things, events and people around them. After all, every thought is a thought 'of something', every feeling a feeling 'of something'. This fundamental and very physical 'involvement' in the concrete, outside world is expressed by the concept of 'intentionality'.[17]

This is the core idea or the 'fait primitif' of existential phenomenology. The starting point of existential phenomenology is, therefore, the lived experience of people. It does not attempt to explain a particular phenomenon out of already existing ideas or some abstract theory. Its intention is to develop a theory 'from the bottom up' and not 'from the top down'. It looks at events and experience from within the concrete context of human life. It is exactly from there that our theory of a lived and embodied spirituality has also been developed.

---

[16] A central characteristic of existential phenomenology is that it provides a way of investigating how, in their daily life, people experience a particular phenomenon. It seeks to understand the essential characteristics of that phenomenon by looking at it from different perspectives in order to arrive at its essence.

Existential phenomenology also enables the phenomenon being explored to be connected with other phenomena in the field around it. Its starting point is the lived experience of people. It does not attempt to explain a particular phenomenon out of already existing ideas or theories.

[17] See: Luijpen, W. *(1971) Nieuwe inleiding tot de existentiële fenomenologie*, Utrecht/Antwerp: Spectrum, 93.

Existential phenomenologists wanted to break away from the dualism between a thinking ego (the 'res cogitans') and a world outside (the 'res extensa'). For a philosopher such as Descartes the human body is part of the 'res extensa', the world outside, and it is therefore an object among other objects.

However, according to Merleau-Ponty it is precisely our body that makes our contact with the world possible. We do not 'have' our body as an instrument for our actions, but 'are' our bodies. The body is a body-subject (in French: *corps-sujet*), a body lived by the subject (Fr: *corps-vécu*). The human being *is* his body and it is through the body and its sensory sensations that people experience the world around them and live in it. The distance they perceive between the body and the world is illusory.

According to Merleau-Ponty, the dualism between body and mind, and between ourselves and the world which was introduced and consolidated in the thinking of Rene Descartes, is philosophically and practically an untenable position. This thinking created a radical and dramatic disconnection between the existence of the subject and the reality outside of him.[18]

In Merleau-Ponty's way of thinking, the human being is 'submerged in his body and entangled in his world'. Merleau-Ponty's idea of 'being' a body underscores the concept of sensory-sensitive bodily experience, which was introduced in Chapter Three. In fact, in his line of thinking, it seems that the functional-instrumental experience of the body is actually absorbed into the sensory-sensitive way of being and living in the world.

Incarnation, centring and transcendence in existential phenomenology

We will now look at the way in which the concepts of incarnation, centring and transcendence emerge from within existential phenomenology. In Chapter Eight, we will describe how this philosophical thinking relates to the way that patients experience their body, gaining a deeper understanding of it. We will do this in connection with the thinking that underlies the practices of Qi Gong and hesychasm, described in the next two chapters.

---

[18] Merleau-Ponty, M. (1945) *Phénoménologie de la perception*. Paris: Galimard.

Incarnation

Whilst the 'being-a-body' of human beings is emphasised by Merleau-Ponty, then it is the mortality of this 'being-a-body', and the resulting awareness of finitude, that play a crucial role within Heidegger's philosophy.[19] This awareness is closely related to our corporeality, i.e. the way in which we are a being-in-a-body.

According to Heidegger, this awareness of mortality is barely present in the consciousness of modern man. Only when confronted with our own death do we realise that, as human beings, we are 'incarnated' in a body that is vulnerable and mortal. Being incarnated in a body is in Heidegger's language *zum Tode sein*—being unto death. Literally, this means that death is an essential aspect of the human condition and fundamentally defines our lives, even when we are not aware of it.

According to Heidegger, as modern human beings, we cannot tolerate the idea of this *zum Tode sein* and the instinctive reaction is to expel death from our conscious minds. Death becomes an abstraction, nothing more than some abstract knowledge. It is something that happens to others and occurs beyond the horizon of our own lives.

By banishing death from daily consciousness, we repress the basic fact that we are incarnated in a mortal body. We are, therefore, always running from who and what we actually are in our essence. Because we are not truly incarnated in our physical and mortal reality, our life dissipates into superficiality and triviality.

According to Heidegger, this is reflected in the all-pervasive futile hassle and 'chatter' (in German: *Gerede*). He calls this way of living *Verfallen (depraved)* and in this state, we live our lives as *one of them*, i.e. one of the masses (German: *das Man*). As 'one of them' we are never really ourselves, that is, never an 'I-self' (German: *Ich-selbst)*, an authentic subject.

Centring

Heidegger sees the confrontation with death as a decisive moment in our psychological development. When we have to look death in the face, we are confronted with the harsh reality of life itself and 'of the possibility of not-being'.

---

[19] Heidegger, M. (1963) *Sein und Zeit,* 10de druk. Tübingen: Max Niemeyer Verlag.

We are thrown back onto our naked self. This is an intense existential shock that calls for heroic endurance and, with it, an acceptance of the fear of death. Learning to live with this fear is the ultimate challenge of our existence.

According to Heidegger, this confrontation with death provides an extraordinary opportunity to get in touch with who we really are. When we discover that we have fallen out of the banal life as 'one of them', then we must give up the illusion of an invulnerable corporeality and the notion that there is endless time for living. It is at such a moment that we descend into the true reality of our body. It is only then that we are truly incarnated and become a true 'I-self'.

The term 'centring' does not occur as such in Heidegger's writings. Yet, where he writes about recapturing contact with the 'I-self', this can be seen as a form of 'centring'. For Heidegger, this does not have a concrete physical meaning—something which is clearly evident in Qi Gong and hesychasm—but a psychological one.

In so far as the 'I-self' can be located in a specific place in the body, then it would be in the middle of the chest, the place we point to with our finger when we say 'I'. In the line of thinking of Heidegger's existential phenomenology, becoming an 'I-self' (Ich-selbst) in the face of death is the ultimate existential task. It is in this 'I-self' that we become centred.

Transcendence

The concept of transcendence points to the movement that takes us beyond the ego-centric focus on ourselves alone. According to existential phenomenology, such a focus is actually impossible because we are not a 'res cogitans', totally separated from the world and others. Rather, we are, from the very depths of our bodies, 'intentionally' involved in the world around us. As already indicated above, every thought, feeling and action shifts the ego-centric focus and takes us, as human beings, out of ourselves into the world beyond.

To existential phenomenologists, the concept of *transcendence* has never meant striving to elevate ourselves above the reality of this world. This is especially true for Merleau-Ponty and Sartre. They offer no vision of an abstract, all-embracing cosmic reality, let alone a god. Existential phenomenologists focused on the reality of the visible and physically tangible world. The thinking of the existentialist philosophers does not seek to go beyond the limit of what is tangibly 'real'. Death is and remains the ultimate limit of life and is its antithesis.

According to them, this world has its very own value as a field of action and self-realisation. In this field, we freely determine our own life. According to existential phenomenologists, we are always attempting to transcend the given conditions of our lives, creating culture and making history.

Criticism of the perspective of existential phenomenology

An important critic of the thinking of the existential phenomenologists was Levinas[20]. He argued that in their thinking there was no room for what is essentially 'other'. It is precisely this otherness, i.e. this 'alterity' that has the potential to break through the familiar and trusted frame of reference which gives meaning to life and defines its horizon. Levinas challenges the phenomenologists' notion of a mundane, down-to-earth perspective of reality. He calls this a form of a finite *horizontal immanence*.

The experiences of the patients we interviewed showed that not all of these can be understood from a strictly finite horizontal-immanent perspective. Experiences of transcendence, such as *infinite space, energy* and *light,* described at the end of the previous chapter, do not figure in the thinking, nor in the experiences of the existentialist philosophers. The philosophers speak of 'being *in*-the-body' or even 'being-*a*-body'.

However, our patients actually discovered deeper dimensions of embodiment, in this 'being-a-body'. Within the terms of existentialist phenomenology, they are more deeply 'submerged' into their body and more deeply 'entangled' with the tangible world around them. And yet, the experience of their body extends beyond that which is only tangibly 'real'.

The experiential world of some of the patients has a very different ring to that of atheistic existentialism, of which Merleau-Ponty and Sartre were staunch

---

[20] Emmanuel Levinas was a French-Jewish philosopher who was born in Lithuania in 1906. After his death in 1995, his work became more popular, especially in the Benelux. His main work from 1961 was *Totality and Infinity* in which he formulated not only his criticism of Existential Phenomenology, but of a general tendency in Western thinking. According to him, 'the other' was always subordinated to the individual's own interests. He emphasized the essential and inalienable 'alterity' of the Other who deserves deep respect.

representatives. The patients' experiences of transcendence seem to confirm Levinas' criticism of existential phenomenology, which he considers to be too exclusively focused on the finite horizontal-immanent dimension of life. The experiences of infinite space, energy and light were so remarkable for our patients that they were genuinely surprised by them.

This surprise is not only a sign of the unusual reality of these experiences but also of their 'alterity', their 'otherness'. These experiences did not fall within the patients' former and familiar frame of reference, which had previously defined their world.

Reflection regarding embodied spirituality

Despite Levinas' criticism, the thinking of existential phenomenology has great value for understanding a significant part of our patients' experiences. It does justice to the body in its vulnerability, to the reality of mortality and the fear of death. It points to those moments of confrontation when we have to face the bare reality of our existence.

In doing this, we are given a chance to become an authentic, even courageous 'I-self'. It is in confronting our mortality that we do justice to the finite immanent dimension of Reality. According to existential phenomenology, accepting and engaging with this confrontation is the ultimate existential challenge. Our patients fully recognised this, whilst at the same time experiencing transcendent moments involving infinite space, light and energy which extended beyond the immanent horizon. This means that immanent and transcendent dimensions were both very much part of their Reality and co-existed simultaneously.

As the experience of transcendence does not figure in the existentialist philosophers' horizontal-immanent view of reality, in the next two chapters, we will examine frameworks that do more justice to these experiences. These frameworks are the practice of Qi Gong within Chinese Daoism and that of hesychasm within Eastern Orthodox Christianity.

Chapter Six
The Perspective of Qi Gong

Reality of infinity: the experience of being part of a 'larger whole'

In this chapter, we describe the practice of Qi Gong within Chinese Daoism and give a brief explanation of the concepts 'Qi' and 'Gong'. We then explain the place which the body occupies within Daoism in a process of spiritual development. In doing this, we hope to show how Qi Gong is a form of a truly *physically* lived spirituality that focuses primarily on valuing earthly reality and is not about striving towards some 'higher realms'.

More than most other spiritual traditions, Qi Gong puts great importance on the very concrete and down-to-earth aspects of human life such as food, landscape, design and layout of the house, physical and psychological health and sexuality. In this description of Qi Gong, we show how the concepts of *incarnation, centring* and *transcendence* have a special and unique content.

Moreover, in Qi Gong, these three concepts are not seen as separate from each other but as a coherent whole. In describing the practice of Qi Gong from the perspectives of incarnation, centring and transcendence, a framework crystallises in which the more 'unusual', transcendent experiences of our patients can be valued and interpreted.

Origin of the Qi Gong practice within Chinese Daoism

The essence of Chinese culture and spirituality manifests itself in the practice of Qi Gong.[21] The essential elements of Qi Gong have ancient roots, being found in the Yi Jing (I Ching), the Book of Changes, a written record (c.700 BC) based

---

[21] Qi Gong. This is the pinyin transliteration of the Chinese characters 气功. The pronunciation in English is Chee Gung.

on an oral tradition, passed down over many centuries. The philosophy of this tradition is attributed to the legendary Yellow Emperor (Huang Di), who is said to have lived between 2690 and 2590 BC.

In the ancient and basic text of Daoïsm, known as the Dao De Jing (道德经) which is attributed to Lao Zi (老子),[22] a number of breathing techniques were already incorporated which aim to increase the vitality of the human body and prolong the lifespan. Zhuang Zi (庄子), an adherent of Daoism, extended these exercises, emphasising the intrinsic connection between breath, energy and health. The arrival of Buddhism in China and the practice of the Qi Gong by Buddhist monks brought about further refinement and a deepening of these exercises.

Qi Gong embodies the characteristic Chinese pursuit of *a balance* between the poles of the Yin and the Yang and of *harmony* between man and nature. It situates the human person in the centre between heaven (*tian* 天) and earth (*di* 地). From this middle position, the human being is part of a large cosmic whole which encompasses everything and all living beings.

For the Qi Gong practitioner, this is not treated as a philosophical concept but points to an experiential reality in which the energies flowing from heaven and earth are truly experienced within the very depths of the human body. This energetic flow forms not only a basic condition for the physical and mental health of the individual, but also impacts on the overall well-being of human society.

What is Qi (气)?

There is no exact equivalence in Western language for the term Qi. This concept, which lies at the essence of Chinese thinking, can easily be disregarded as something elusive or 'vague' because of the difficulty in finding an adequate equivalent definition and translation. This highlights a fundamental problem in the dialogue between Eastern and Western thinking. From the time of the Greek philosophers, Western thinking has pursued exactness in its formulations and concepts, whilst Chinese thinking allows for much more fluidity and complexity in the use of certain words and concepts.

---

[22] Lao Zi is said to have lived in the 6th century BC, but the current scientific view is that Lao Zi should be considered a mythological figure. The Dao De Jing attributed to him is the most basic text of Daoism.

The well-known Dutch sinologist, Kristof Schipper, writes that probably the first meaning of Qi was 'steam' or 'vapour', but also 'breath'. Hence, through the concept of breath, it was identified with the life force and the spirit of the body.[23] In most literature about Qi Gong, Qi is seen as the life energy that permeates the entire universe and all beings living within it.[24]

According to Schipper, the term Qi can be compared with the Sanskrit concept of *prana* or with the Greek *pneuma*. He indicates that the original meaning of the latter is *breath, air, wind* and *life force*. In other languages, there are also words that express the same all-pervasive, cosmic-energetic reality, such as the Hebrew *ruach* (meaning spirit, wind) or the Latin *spiritus* (spirit).

What is Gong (功)?

Gong is the abbreviated form of the word Gongfu (功夫) and means 'work', in the sense of a sustained and committed effort to achieve a desired goal. Qi Gong means steady and patient practice for the sake of being able to optimise the energetic flow within the body. Because human beings are embedded within the great cycles of nature, it is of the utmost importance that they follow 'the way of nature' or the way of the Dao (道). When they deviate from this path, they become derailed, 'lose their balance, get sick, die and fall apart'.[25]

This embeddedness within nature and the cosmos as a whole means that human beings must take into account the many factors that affect them: climatic and geographical conditions, impact of the seasons, time of day, quality of food, construction and furnishing of the house (called *feng shui* 风 水), etc. Human health can be promoted by understanding the influence and interdependence of these factors and by channelling the Qi in and through the body. There is a spaciousness within Chinese thought which allows for this complexity in life to be seen and acknowledged. For this reason, it is very difficult to identify a single causal relationship between one of these factors with a particular disease, as many factors are interdependent and work together.

---

[23] Schipper, K. (1988) *Tao, de levende religie van China.* Amsterdam: Meulenhof, 7. (original title: *Le Corps Taoist,* Paris: Librairie Arthème Fayard).

[24] Yang, J. M. (1989) *The Root of Chinese Chi Kung: The Secrets of Chi Kung Training,* 2nd edition. Jamaica Plain, Massachusetts, USA: YMA, A Publication Center, 6.

[25] Yang, 6.

Within Daoism, more than in many other religious or spiritual movements, the body and mind are seen as intimately connected. Daoism involves a lived spirituality that is naturally rooted in physicality and not marked by a dualistic view of reality.[26]

This means that the function of the body, in the process of spiritual development, is very different from that in more dualistically oriented religious movements. In dualistic-spiritual traditions, the body is often seen as an obstacle to spiritual development which must be rigorously controlled or even completely 'eliminated' by means of all kinds of ascetic techniques. In Daoism, the body is expressly 'involved' in spiritual development and systematically cultivated to support this. Kristof Schipper writes that the earlier mentioned philosopher Zhuang Zi[27] even made the statement that Daoism is 'a religion of the body'.

Within Daoism, the connection between body and mind has always remained intact and has developed into an extraordinary and sometimes very intricate perspective on the human body. Daoism does not look at the body as a collection of anatomical components, but as a microcosmic reflection of the macrocosm. The body does not stand outside or in opposition to the cosmos, but is intimately connected with it.

Cosmic energies penetrate the very fibres, organs, cells and energy channels (meridians) of this body, which, in its essence, forms part of the surrounding reality: nature, the world and the cosmos. That is why individual human beings not only have a duty and a responsibility to care for their own bodies, but are also called to make a contribution to the well-being of the community in which they live and to the world around them.

The aim of the process in spiritual development, as advocated by Daoism, transcends individualistic, ego-centred well-being. Its aim is to view humankind

---

[26] Daoism is not the only spiritual movement in which the body plays a crucial role. Examples of other movements are Shamanism and Tantric Vajrayana Buddhism in the Tibetan tradition.

[27] Zhuang Zi is said to have lived from 369–286 BC. He is a poetic-anarchist thinker and an opponent of closed social and philosophical systems with their claim to what is true and real. His starting point is that 'not-being', 'not-knowing' and 'not-doing' is the basis of our reality, knowing and acting. The texts he left are among the oldest Daoist writings and have had a major influence on the culture of China, Korea and Japan.

as an inclusive whole. Schipper argues that Daoism is profoundly humanistic and is ultimately about the generation, the birth and growth of the 'True Man' (Chin. *zhen ren*: 真人).

Balance in body, soul and spirit as the essence of Qi Gong practice

The essence of Qi Gong practice is the creation of a dynamic balance between apparently opposite poles. This same striving for balance is something we have already described in Chapter Three when we explored the balance between the functional-instrumental and sensory-sensitive experiences of the body. Within Qi Gong, this process is not described in these psychological terms but in energetic terms, which include physical, as well as psychic and even cosmic aspects. On the basis of this energetic terminology, a very dynamic picture emerges of a constant and lively interaction between opposite poles.[28]

In the following section, we highlight this search for a balance between seemingly very opposite forces, as pursued within Daoism. We examine this in some detail because it is this search for balance which forms a 'Leitmotif' in the process of a lived and embodied spirituality.

Describing the opposing forces in the terminology of Qi Gong may sound rather esoteric and is an example of how a dialogue between two very different worlds of thought is challenging, calling for patience and a 'willingness to listen'.

Water and fire: balance between water Qi and fire Qi

For a proper understanding of the functioning of the Qi in the human body, it is important to know the distinction between two types of Qi, which actually appear to be extreme opposites of each other. The first is the Qi that a person receives through his parents and ancestors before birth. This is called the 'original' or 'ancestral Qi' (*xian tian qi*: 先天气). The second is the Qi that is absorbed during daily life through nutrition, proper breathing and lifestyle (*hou tian qi*: 后天气).

---

[28] Finding balance and interaction between apparently totally different significant entities (God and wo/man!) is something that will be returned to in the chapter on hesychasm.

The fact that opposing forces are involved becomes clearer when one knows that in Chinese terminology the original Qi is called 'water Qi' (*shui qi:* 水 气*)* and the second 'fire Qi' (*huo qi:* 火 气).

The 'water Qi' thrives in a situation of relaxation, peace and contentment. The 'fire Qi' flares up due to the tension that can arise from passions and desires. It is characteristic of Chinese thinking that these two types of Qi are located at specific places in the body.

The water Qi is located in the space of the lower abdomen and pelvis. The energetic centre in this area is called the *lower Dan Tian* (*xia dantian:* 下丹田). The fire Qi is located higher in the body, in the area of the solar plexus and the heart. It is the transition from the lower body (pelvic area) to the upper body (breast and head). The centre here is called the *middle Dan Tian* (*zhong dantian:* 中丹田).[29]

In Qi Gong practice, great importance is attached to balancing the water Qi in the lower body and the fire Qi in the stomach area and thus connecting the spaces of the lower body and the upper body into one whole. When this happens, a person is more of a whole and his/her vital energy can flow optimally through the entire body.[30] The circulation of this energy within the body promotes psycho-physical health and supports recovery from illness.

The balance between water Qi and fire Qi is another way of describing the balance that is to be found in the body and which is widely known these days as the poles of Yin (阴) and Yang (阳). This is the great polarity which permeates the entirety of Chinese thinking. The interplay of Yin and Yang also forms the foundation of traditional Chinese medicine.[31] It is important not to see Yin and Yang as totally opposed to each other. In fact, they interact and complement each other. Yin always contains an element of Yang, and Yang of Yin.

---

[29] An upper *Dan Tian* is also distinguished, namely the point between the eyebrows, the so-called Yin Tang point. In the body of acupuncture literature, this point is said to promote a clearer view of reality.

[30] Mantak & Maneewan Chia's extensive and very comprehensible cycle of energy and inner light is described in: *Awaken Healing Light of the Tao,* (New York: Huntington, 1992), 169–172.

[31] Macioca, G. (1989) *The Foundations of Chinese Medicine: A Comprehensive Text for Acupuncturists and Herbalists.* New York: Churchill Livingstone.

In Qi Gong practice, this thinking has crystallised into a range of psycho-physical exercises so that these polar energies can be regulated and balanced. In this way, they can be used in the service of physical, psychological and spiritual health. Because the relationship between body and mind always was a natural part of Daoism, Qi Gong has developed a very refined energetic 'experiential expertise', something which has never been developed in the West.

This interplay between fire Qi and water Qi can be compared with the interaction and complementary effect of the sympathetic and parasympathetic nervous system, as recognised in Western neurology. The fire Qi has a similar function to the sympathetic nervous system, which has an activating effect and is switched on in stress situations (fight-or-flight response). The water Qi can be compared with the parasympathetic nervous system, which has a damping down effect and is switched on in the organism during the rest-recovery state.

This shows that despite the completely different terminology, there is a similar logic regarding the healthy balanced functioning of the bodily organism between traditional Chinese and modern Western thinking.

Incarnation, centring and transcendence within Qi Gong practice

We can now look at the three aspects of bodily experience which came to the fore whilst we were reflecting on the experiences of the patients in Chapter Four: *incarnation, centring* and *transcendence*. The integration of these three aspects of bodily experience will now be described within the context of Qi Gong practice.

Incarnation

The phrase 'down to earth' characterises the fundamental focus of Chinese culture. Its spirituality has always been strongly focused on earthly reality, where the earth is never the valley of tears, as often presented in Christianity. This 'earthliness' in Chinese spirituality never aims for that kind of separation between body and mind, whereby the 'pure' mind has to detach itself from the 'impure' and sin-inclined body. This was often the tendency in the thinking of the Christian West, where it was influenced by Neo-Platonism and Gnosis.

In spiritual development within Chinese culture, a broadening and deepening contact with the body is always implied. Spiritual processes are not seen as separate from the body but as something that need to be 'grounded' and *incarnated* in the body. A discipline of bodily awareness, physical exercise and a certain way of breathing is considered necessary for this.

The first condition for developing this type of contact with the body involves deep physical relaxation, because the mind can only anchor itself in a body that is relaxed and, therefore, open and receptive. It is only in a state of 'open receptivity' that the Qi flows freely through the energy channels (the meridians) of the body. The relaxation that is pursued goes beyond the forms of relaxation that are practiced in various Western relaxation techniques. It is not just about relaxing muscles, but about relaxing deeply into the organs of the body, even into the marrow of the bones and the pores of the skin.

Incarnation by creating a balance between water Qi and fire Qi

To achieve this deep relaxation, the mind must be in balance and not disturbed by the restless 'fire Qi' that flashes up in the area of the solar plexus and the heart region and runs through the entire body. This corresponds with the harmful effect of an over-stimulated sympathetic nervous system due to a prolonged state of stress. The unrest caused by fire Qi disturbs the peace that is necessary to keep a person's connection with the earth intact and prevents him or her from being truly present in the body.

The Chinese term for the restless state of mind that is controlled by the fire Qi is *Xin* (literally 'heart' 心). The term for the state of mind controlled by the water Qi is *Yi* (wisdom 意). The *Xin*-spirit which acts under the influence of the fire Qi is ruled by the passions, ambitions, all sorts of sympathies and antipathies.[32] The *Yi*-spirit which is under the influence of the water Qi represents inner peace, wise judgment and a positively focused power of the will. In the terminology of Western neurology, the *Yi*-spirit stands for the calming and balancing effect of the parasympathetic nervous system.

The passions which arise out of the *Xin*-spirit focus on achieving goals in the future and in the outside world. In Chapter Three, we said that this drive is characteristic of the functional-instrumental way of experiencing the body.

---

[32] This description of the *Xin*-spirit is very similar to the sympathetic nervous system and to our description of the functional-instrumental body experience explored in Chapter Three. The localization of the *Xin*-spirit in the plexus Solaris and the role that the passions play in it can be seen as an addition to this description.

Interviews with our patients suggested that this is the dominant experience of their body before they became ill.

When people are connected with the *Yi*-spirit, they are more focused on actual experiences in the body without them being coloured by personal emotions and prejudices.[33] This is in line with the sensory-sensitive experience of the body that manifests itself ever more strongly during and after the disease process.

Even though for most people the passionate fire Qi of the *Xin*-spirit needs to be tempered, it is not a question of eliminating the *Xin*-spirit completely and only cultivating a *Yi*-spirit. Balancing *Xin* and *Yi* (fire Qi and water Qi) is a basic principle in Qi Gong practice. This reflects the balance that must exist in all areas of life between Yang and Yin.

When the poles of *Xin* and *Yi* are in balance with each other, a person is psychologically balanced and is able to live his life naturally and to act with agency. Both poles complement each other and must therefore remain intact and integrated with each other. It is the same logic that points to the necessary interaction between the sympathetic and parasympathetic nervous systems.

Yet, in Chinese thinking it is deemed important that the *Xin*-spirit, driven by the passions, must conform to the *Yi*-spirit of peace and wisdom and be embedded in this. The *Xin*-spirit tends to pull people towards a state of over activity and too far away from their own body. The *Yi*-spirit leads people back to this.

In pursuing this balance between fire Qi (*Xin*) and water Qi (*Yi*), there is not only a correspondence between the balance that needs to exist between the sympathetic and the parasympathetic nervous system, but also between the functional-instrumental and sensory sensitive experiences of the body described in Chapter Three. This implies a healthy balance between outward-directed activity and a more sensory-sensitive state that remains embedded in the body. Incarnation exists by virtue of this balance, which is not a static but a dynamic equilibrium.

We have seen that when patients reach the end of their period of illness, this balance can manifest itself in different modes and at different levels. We concluded in Chapter Four that striving for and hopefully finding such a balance forms an essential dynamic of a lived and an embodied spirituality. The balance

---

[33] This description of the 'Yi-spirit' corresponds to our description of the sensory-sensitive body experience and shows an additional aspect to it.

being pursued in Qi Gong practice corroborates this kind of spirituality and translates it in terms of energetic processes.

Centring

Essential to Qi Gong practice is the development of a form of bodily awareness in which the centre of gravity lies within the space of the pelvis in the middle of the body. The importance attached to the experience of this bodily centre reflects the position that is ascribed to human beings in the Chinese worldview: that people live between earth and heaven. It is not from the head that the Chinese philosophically 'thinks' about his or her place in the cosmos in a rational way, but actually 'experiences' this place from the middle of the body.

As indicated above, the area of the lower abdomen and pelvis is the place where the water Qi is located and where the spirit of wisdom (*Yi*) thrives, bringing inner peace and insight into the great cycles of nature, life and cosmos. This spirit of wisdom brings the insight that human beings are part of this cycle. Being centred in the middle of the body and at the same time open to earth, heaven and cosmos indicates the intimate movement between becoming centred and being more open to a transcendent dimension.

In Qi Gong, many exercises have been developed to anchor bodily consciousness in this centre of the body. Fundamental to this is the need to cultivate:

1. Deeper breathing
2. Relaxation of the passions
3. The bringing together of opposite poles

- *Cultivating deeper breathing*

Deeper relaxation and a deepening of the breath are closely related. Increasing numbers of people have learned first-hand how stress impacts directly on their daily life and on the way they breathe. Our breathing becomes more restless, irregular and rises to a higher level in the chest.[34] The deep state of

---

[34] This is also well-known in various Western schools of breathing therapy, in particular those of Alice Schaarschuch, Ilse Middendorf, Hetty Draayer. This breathing higher up

relaxation that Qi Gong practice brings about means that breathing becomes calmer, more regular and deeper.

In Qi Gong practice, it is emphasised that this deeper breathing must occur naturally, as 'of itself'. The breath is not controlled by the will or consciously regulated. This is very different from most Pranayama breathing techniques in Indian yoga. In the more unconstrained Daoist way of breathing, the Chinese ideal of *Wu Wei* (无为) emerges: non-doing.

This does not mean 'doing nothing', but 'doing' by allowing the natural process to take place and by not interfering with this. The intended ideal is like that of the natural breathing of a new-born child. Then, without any force, abdominal breathing occurs. This is the key for being able to access the energy reservoir in the centre of the body in the space of the pelvis. This is the lower *Dan Tian* (*xia dantian:* 下丹田), wherein lies the source of vitality, energy and life force.

- *Relaxation of the passions*

'The silence of the heart' is a condition necessary for further discovering this centre. For the ancient Chinese, the heart was the seat of thinking as ruled by the passions from the *Xin*-spirit. The silence of the heart means that the mind must be calmed and the passions tempered. Only the silence of the heart can remove the barriers between mental consciousness and the body or between the thinking mind and the true experience of the body. In other words, between the over-active *Xin* mind, directed towards the outside world and the calm receptive *Yi* mind, directed towards the inner experience.

According to Chinese practitioners of Qi Gong, the *Xin* (the Yang aspect of the mind) always pursues what is without limit and measure, which leads to a depletion of the life forces. The *Yi* (the Yin aspect of the mind) knows how to maintain a measured response which respects the natural limitations of the body. Thanks to the *Yi*, people can find peace in their heart and anchor themselves in the centre of their body.

---

in the chest is also characteristic of the functional-instrumental body experience described in Chapter Three.

This anchoring in the centre, in the depths of our bodies, brings a concrete physical reality to the concept of *centring*.[35] If we now think about this from the perspective of the functional-instrumental experience of the body and the sensory-sensitive experience (as described in Chapter Three), then the two aspects are intimately connected and need to be in balance for a person to be really centred.

- *The bringing together of opposite poles*

The centre is also activated when the polar energies of the male and female (Yang and Yin) unite in the lower *Dan Tian*. Schipper describes an inner, energetic-alchemical process in which sexual energies also play an important role. This energy is not necessarily directed at fulfilling the sexual act, but is awakened to permeate the entire body. He writes: "The love that is released spreads throughout the entire body and infuses all organs and all functions of the body."[36]

Transcendence

Qi Gong practice can lead to a fundamentally different experience of the body, in which all gravity is dissolved from the physical body, causing it to feel light and transparent. It is an experience whereby the body is no longer perceived as being enclosed within its visible physical bodily contours but as something that is transcending its boundaries and extending into the space around the body.

This occurs because of the widening of the energy field, brought about by the Qi Gong exercises. The Qi in the centre of the body has increased so much that it radiates beyond the skin.[37] This corresponds to the physical experiences of transcendence—of *energy, space* and *light*—described by a number of patients and explored in Chapter Four.

Schipper describes how, in the course of the development of the Qi field, higher and higher centres of consciousness are opened up and reunification with

---

[35] The remarkable similarities between the cultivation of the center of the body and the practice of hesychasm are discussed in the next chapter.

[36] Schipper, 197.

[37] In Chapter Seven we discuss the corresponding pattern of the mandorla around the shape of Christ, as it is depicted on the icons of the Transfiguration on Mount Tabor.

'the Great One' (*Tai Yi*) is ultimately realised. This points to the reality that spiritual development is characterised by different phases, which in Daoism always have a definite physical component in specific parts of the body. Three centres are distinguished within the body: one in the lower area of the body, one in the heart area and one in the centre of the head.

These three centres correspond to three levels of spiritual development. The transition from one level to the other can also be seen as a moment of transcendence within the space of one's own body. The centre in the lower abdomen (*xia dantian*) represents the embryonic phase of spiritual development. When the embryo is fully grown, then the middle area fills itself with Qi.

The centre in the middle of the breast (*zhong dantian*) represents the child phase of spiritual development and is often visualised as the 'baby' being born in the heart. The next phase announces itself when the energy makes the transition from the breast area to the space of the head.

The opening of the centre in the middle of the head (*Yin Tang*: point between and behind the eyebrows) represents the mature phase of spiritual development and the realisation of the 'True Man' (*zhen ren*). It is from the centre in the head that the road is open to unification with the Great One.

This union with the Great One is accompanied by an inner ecstasy, whereby the sexual energy, as described by Schipper, permeates body, soul and spirit as an inner, almost orgasmic sensation and union with the 'Great One' (*Tai Yi*) is realised.

Figure 1 shows the embryonic phase of spiritual development.

Figure 1

The transition from one centre to another is made possible by an exercise called the 'microcosmic orbit' which creates a cycle of energy and light within the body. When a sufficient amount of Qi has collected in the lower *Dan Tian*, this energy can then be directed to different places in the body. A classic way of doing this is to allow the Qi energy to circulate in 'the small orbit', that is, from the centre of the perineum (*Hui Yin* point: 白 会) and then to move upwards along the spine and through the head (along the *Bai Hui* 白 会 point in the middle of the skull) to then move down through the front of the body.

The purpose of this meditative exercise is to integrate body and mind. Two energy channels are of great importance within this cycle: the governor meridian (*du mo*) behind the backbone and the conception meridian (*ren mo*) on the front of the body. The next step is to bring the Qi into 'the great orbit'. Then the energy flows freely through all the limbs, energy channels and organs 'transcending' the skin so that it radiates from inside the body to the space outside.[38]

---

[38] This detailed description of Chinese energy theory also aims to make the energy theory of hesychasm, as visualized in the icon of the Transfiguration, more comprehensible and insightful.

This physical-energetic state of transcendence is, of course, not achieved by many people. In the introduction to this chapter, we described a more basic form of transcendence in which people see themselves as standing in the midst between heaven (*Tian*) and earth (*Di*) and experience themselves as part of nature and the cosmos. Another and a more down-to-earth aspect of transcendence can be seen in the incentive to not only take care of one's own body but also that of our loved ones (family and friends), the environment and the world.

Several patients from groups 1 and 2 reported experiences that were very similar to the transcendent experiences described within Qi Gong practice, such as feeling the flow of energies; experiences of bodily space that extend beyond the contours of the skin; a sense of lightness and even the perception of an inner light. Whilst these were very unusual and inexplicable experiences for the patients, they are understandable and even predictable within the energetic paradigm of Qi Gong.

The fact that people who live in our time and culture have these experiences makes the practice of Qi Gong less strange and esoteric than it initially might appear.

Integrating incarnation, centring and transcendence

What comes to the fore in the above is the importance of the integration of opposite poles (fire Qi and water Qi; *Xin*-spirit and *Yi*-spirit; the sympathetic and parasympathetic nervous systems). Finding such a balance is also essential within the psycho-spiritual process of an embodied spirituality.

Integration in the centre of the body

What the above demonstrates is that in Qi Gong practice, this balance is realised in the centre of the body and very concretely in the space of the lower abdomen and pelvis. This centre is the place where seemingly opposite poles, involving processes of incarnation and transcendence, are actually connected. This is consistent with what we learned from the patients' experiences, namely that *centring* is the connecting link between being both more present in the body and feeling part of a larger whole.

This importance of integrating two opposite poles, although expressed differently, is also described in a text translated by Richard Wilhelm with a commentary by C.G. Jung, entitled *The Secret of the Golden Flower*.[39] This was one of the first texts that introduced Chinese energetic thinking to a larger audience in the West. In the same book, Wilhelm and Jung also published *The Book of Consciousness and Life*. These two Daoist texts stem from the same tradition as Qi Gong and describe in detail the circulation of Qi energy in the human body, described above as the microcosmic orbit.

Wilhelm and Jung state that *The Secret of the Golden Flower* is the inner light that manifests itself in a person when 'the Great One' or Dao has been realised in him. This happens when 'the two have become one', i.e. when Yang and Yin have come into balance with each other. In this text, it becomes clear that this 'unification' involves a physical anchoring in the middle of the body. The inner light reveals itself at first in the inner space of the pelvis and lower abdomen.

In the writing of Wilhelm and Jung, this is called the space of the 'zygote'[40], the germinal vesicle, which is another reference to the aforementioned lower Dantian. This inner light is born in the darkness of this space. In Jung's depth psychological interpretation of this, it means that out of the darkness of this space the unconscious is brought into the light of consciousness. Thus, making contact with this centre involves a process of incarnation in the body which, at the same time, makes possible a moment of real transcendence into an all-embracing reality. It therefore appears that in Qi Gong the three aspects of bodily awareness, *incarnation, centring* and *transcendence* clearly come together and are integrated with each other.

In the second Chinese text, *The Book of Consciousness and Life*, the two poles are translated by Wilhelm as 'life' and 'consciousness'. It is when these are united that an experience of an inner white light arises, that emanates from the centre of the body.[41] The bringing together of these poles is not achieved by

---

[39] Wilhelm, R. and Jung, C. G. (1932) *The Secret of the Golden Flower: A Chinese Book of Life*. New York: Harcourt, Brace & Company. (Original title: *Das Geheimnis der Goldenen Blüte*, (Olten & Freiburg iB: Walter Verlag).)

[40] Zygote refers to a fertilized egg or ovum half contributed by the mother and half by the father. The zygote divides to become an embryo, which continues to divide as it develops and differentiates, eventually becoming a foetus.

[41] This theme of an inner white light emanating from the centre of the body is also recognised in hesychasm as the 'Tabor light', radiating from the centre of the body of Christ into the world around.

willpower or the rational mind. It involves a process of turning inwards into the centre and from there opening up to life in its totality. This involves a process of spiritual development that encompasses the whole person in body, mind and spirit. This process is often visualised in various ways.[42]

Integration of opposites: a process of individuation

The recurring theme in Qi Gong is the merging of two opposites (Fire Qi and Water Qi, *Xin*-spirit and *Yi*-spirit, Yang and Yin).[43] It is because of this that Jung argues that Chinese thinking is much more able than Western thinking of 'keeping the polarity in life, as a paradox, intact'.

According to Jung, this bringing together of seemingly opposite poles involves a process of individuation. In Qi Gong, this is referred to as the realisation of the 'true man' (*zhen ren*). In this, Qi Gong provides a context for statements by patients who say: "Now I am finally the person who I really am." The echo of Heidegger's words on becoming a real 'I-self' (Ich selbst) can be heard, but in Qi Gong philosophy it takes on a much deeper and wider dimension.

Wu Wei is the key to comprehending the paradox of opposite poles existing together. As we saw earlier, *Wu Wei* refers to 'doing by not doing' so that natural processes are able to take place. Jung compares this *Wu Wei* with the 'sich lassen' of Meister Eckhart whereby life can evolve 'out of itself'.

In the words of Jung, embracing the paradox of life means "raising the level of consciousness, expanding, elevating and enriching the personality." He regards the capacity of being able to embrace the full paradox of life as the essence of the process of 'individuation': the process of becoming who you

---

[42] In the Chinese texts on this topic there are various and often for us rather unfathomable, images to be found. Jung recognises in these images the basic pattern of the mandala as a 'map' of spiritual development in which fundamental polarities are profoundly connected with each other. In the description of the icon of the Transfiguration in the next chapter, we will once again encounter the motif of the mandala.

[43] In addition to the balance between the sympathetic and parasympathetic nervous system and the functional-instrumental and sensory-sensitive experience of the body, there is in western thinking also the recognition of the need for balance between the function of the right and the left hemispheres of the brain. The cooperation between these seemingly opposite poles are necessary for the adequate functioning of the human being.

really are.[44] In the final chapter, we attempt to flesh out the expression 'becoming who you are', as an essential aspect of contemporary lived and embodied spirituality.

The limitations in the perspective of Qi Gong

This perspective from Qi Gong provides a framework in which the more 'unusual' transcendent experiences of patients, with regard to the processes of *incarnation, centring* and *transcendence,* find recognition and—although within a completely different system of thinking—become somewhat more understandable. An important limitation, however, is that the more 'ordinary' experiences of the patients, such as being aware of their own limits and mortality, the fear of death, the loss of future, meaning and identity, do not occur in Qi Gong literature.

This is because in the practice of Qi Gong, the Chinese focus is primarily on physical health, longevity and even physical immortality. An extreme example of this is that the Chinese emperors often forced their alchemists to make a pill from herbs and rare metals which would make them immortal. Taking such a pill seems to have resulted in the death of Qin Shi Huang Di, the first emperor of China, because of the amount of mercury in it.

This takes suppression of the reality of death to the highest level! We saw in the previous chapter that within the domain of existential phenomenology (Heidegger), becoming aware of our mortality provides the ultimate opportunity for us to become a subject, a real 'I-self'. This opportunity seems to be lost on the Qi Gong practitioner.

Neglecting the process of becoming a subject, i.e. a unique and real 'I-self', is something that Qi Gong has in common with many other Eastern traditions of spirituality which emphasise letting go of the ego. Rather, the ideal involves the merging of the self with the universe. This Eastern form of spirituality can be seen in many Western 'New Age' movements that have been on the rise in recent

---

[44] Wilhelm, 80. At this juncture, Jung draws the paradox to a climax by citing the following words from the apostle Paul: *And it is no longer I who live, but it is Christ who lives in me.* (Gal. 2:20). According to Jung, *in the Pauline symbol of Christ the highest religious experiences of the West and the East touch each other. Christ, the hero full of sorrows and the golden flower—what a contradiction, what a wide gap between both traditions! A problem, fit for the masterpiece of a future psychology.*

decades. The 'ego' is regarded as the major obstacle on the road to enlightenment. There is little appreciation of the uniqueness of each person and the concrete involvement with other people and the world around.

Despite the preoccupation with long life and immortality, human life (in Daoist thought) is undeniably embedded in the great cycles of nature. Much more than modern Western people, the Daoist experiences him/herself as part of a larger whole, as a microcosm within the macrocosm. This means that the natural cycle of birth and death has not been completely erased from Chinese consciousness. The connection between life and death lies at the very foundation in the meaning structure of their culture.

When the patients spoke about suddenly 'feeling part of a larger whole', this seems to equate with the same experience as that of Qi Gong practitioners. Yet, the path to such an experience is a very different one and perhaps also determines the nature of the experience itself. Whilst the experience of being embedded within the greater whole of life and death lies at the foundation of the meaning structure of Chinese culture, the confrontation with mortality for our patients marks a dramatic break in the meaning structure which, until that moment, governed their lives.

This is why in many cases this confrontation leads to an existential crisis, 'a dark night of the soul'. In Heidegger's terms, it is a fall out of 'das Man'. But according to him, this confrontation with the finitude of life gives Western people a unique opportunity to become a true 'Ich selbst' (I-self).

In order to do justice to the two truths, namely that of the reality of human mortality and the paradoxical experience of infinity that several patients also perceived, we will now turn to the perspective of hesychasm. In this ancient, but little known tradition in Western Christianity, we shall discover an acknowledgement and frame of reference for these two truths.

Chapter Seven
The Perspective of Hesychasm

The reality of paradox: living in a finite and infinite Reality

We now introduce and describe hesychasm, a unique and interesting movement within Eastern Orthodox Christianity. In this ancient Christian tradition, the body was assigned a special place in the spiritual development of the person. During our exploration of hesychasm we will also acquaint ourselves with the 'icon' as a material, physical reality representing something that is immaterial and spiritual. Within Eastern Orthodox spirituality, icons have a special place.

A deeper theological vision of the true meaning of icons was developed in response to the iconoclasm which raged through the Christian East in the ninth century and led to the destruction of nearly all material, religious images made of stone and paint. In this vision, the relationship between body and spirit, between material reality and spiritual reality and ultimately between the human person and God was fundamentally worked out.

It is especially the Tabor icon, which depicts Jesus Christ in his transfigured state 'on a high mountain' that makes the spirituality of hesychasm clearly visible and tangible. It is by means of this icon that we will again visit the three central themes that we introduced in Chapter Four, of incarnation, centring and transcendence. Doing this will help to throw further light on some of the remarkable experiences of our patients.

Origins of hesychasm within Eastern Orthodox Christianity

In the Western world, hesychasm is a lesser known form of spirituality. It is rooted in Eastern Orthodox Christianity and its beginnings go back to the fourth century. Initially, it was practiced exclusively by monks who lived as hermits in the deserts of the Near East or in small monastic communities within the Sinai desert.

Both Qi Gong and hesychasm confront us with terms and concepts which are rooted in the context of a particular time and a different culture. Even though the terms and concepts in hesychasm are essentially Christian, and possibly more familiar to us than those of Chinese Daoism, our increasingly secular society means that they have become less familiar and may provoke resistance rather than curiosity.

As with Qi Gong, a 'willingness to listen' to the language of hesychasm is needed, so that the underlying meaning can be discovered. Whilst hesychasm provides a window for viewing, understanding and valuing the experiences of the patients, these experiences can shed light on the 'strangeness' of hesychasm, so that its spirituality can be valued and understood.

Hesychia

The term hesychasm is derived from the Greek word *hesychia* (ἡσυχία) which means quiet, rest and solitude. In the isolation of monasteries and deserts, monks sought out the physical conditions which would lead to the deep inner peace and quietude of *hesychia*. *Hesychia* is something that needs to be anchored in a deep peace of mind, freedom from passions and disturbing thoughts, i.e. freedom from the 'ego'.

An important means for arriving at this place is the practice of inner vigilance (in Greek: νῆψις, *nepsis*), being alert and 'mindful' to the thoughts, emotions and bodily sensations that disturb inner peace. In the space that then opens up, God can gain access to the innermost person. The essential condition for this involves emptying the mind of the many disturbing, exalted, beautiful and positive thoughts. The aim is to create a mind that is completely empty of all thoughts and emotions ('νοῦς γυμνός', nous gumnos).

Through certain meditative techniques, such as focusing attention and directing their breath towards the centre of their bodies, monks sought complete union with God. They hoped that the divine light would eventually reveal itself from within. In this focusing of attention and breathing in the centre of the body, a remarkable similarity emerges with the practice of Qi Gong. It is as if the Near East approaches the Far East.

Part of this spiritual practice involved the constant repetition of a short and simple prayer that would eventually become part of the very heart and soul of the monk. This prayer was silently spoken in the cadence of breathing in and breathing out. The words of this prayer (the so-called Jesus prayer) were: *Jesus Christ, Son of God, have mercy on us.*

When breathing in, the monk would silently say the words *Jesus Christ, Son of God* and when breathing out those of *have mercy on us.* Variations to this were also possible, such as a single line from the Gospel or the Psalms. This form of prayer was first and foremost about simplicity so that the turmoil of the mind could, as it were, be blocked and brought to a point of stillness.

In this way, an inner space could open up which would extend beyond the noise of all discursive thoughts and emotions. The famous Russian theologian Paul Evdokimov states how the character of prayer essentially changes so that at a given moment the prayer in the monk becomes an autonomous process, so that eventually *the soul prays outside of the prayer.*[45] When a person has purified himself from the maelstrom of all encircling thoughts and passions, God's grace can enter into the inner space of the soul and this presence can be experienced 'as a radiant light'.[46]

This 'radiant light' was eventually seen to be the same light that radiated from Christ at the moment of his transfiguration on Mount Tabor (Mt.17:1–8; Mk.9:2–8; Lk.9:28–36). The monk hoped that one day he would also experience this Tabor light within himself. His entire life was focused on that and to that end he kept his breathing and attention focused on the centre of his body, filling his mind with the words and resonance of the Jesus prayer.

The inner light which is experienced within the practice of *hesychia* clearly resonates with the practice of Qi Gong when the Qi is aroused and circulates within and around the body. This is the moment when a person can experience an inner light, which can be described as a manifestation of 'the Great One' (Tai Yi).

The reality of such an experience of light has not always been undisputed. The question was always, as it remains to this day, whether the experience of an inner light is real or a kind of self-created, self-hypnotic 'religious' ecstasy. In

---

[45] Evdokimov, P. (1959) *L'Orthodoxie*, Neuchatel: Bibliothèque théologique, Delachaux et Netslé SA, 119.

[46] Andreopoulos, A. (2005) *Metamorphosis: The Transfiguration in Byzantine Theology and Iconography*, New York: St. Vladimir's Seminary Press, 214.

the fourteenth century, the reality of this experience was indeed fiercely challenged in the great controversy between Gregory Palamas and Barlaäm of Calabria, to which we will return.

The prerequisite of hesychastic spirituality was ultimately about an undoubted belief in the existence of God and in Jesus Christ as the Son who mediates the relationship between humankind and God. The relevance of this form of spirituality for the interpretation of the experiences of our patients does not lie in the acceptance of certain religious beliefs. Rather, it lies in the experience of tranquillity, in being able to empty the mind of the restless movement of thoughts and emotions and in particular of the experience of an inner light which some of the patients spoke about.

This excursion into hesychasm is particularly about a way of thinking—even in an authentic Christian tradition—that transcends the dualism between body and mind and creates space for experiences of transcendence.

The place of the body within the spirituality of hesychasm

A remarkable facet of hesychasm was the positive role assigned to the body. The beating of the heart and the rhythm of the breath were explicitly involved in the rhythmic repetition of the words of the Jesus prayer. This was one of the ways to make the body part of 'pure prayer' and not to regard it as an obstacle on the way to union with God in the experience of the divine light. John Climacus, who was abbot of the famous St Catherine's Monastery on Mount Sinai in the seventh century, counselled his monks: "The memory of Jesus must become one with your breathing, then you will understand the usefulness of inner quietude."

This positive relationship to the body is remarkable because, as we mentioned earlier, the widespread Neo-Platonic and Gnostic influences in the early days of Christianity had often created a very negative relationship between body and mind.[47] The body was seen as the dungeon of the spirit, with all evil coming from the body.

---

[47] Gnosis (Gr.Υνωσις: knowledge, insight). This was a movement that was already in existence before the emergence of Christianity, especially in Asia Minor. It had its roots in ancient Persian dualistic thinking. A characteristic was the fundamental contrast between light and dark, God and the world. Basilides and Valentinus in particular

The fundamental question that, according to an author like Andreopoulos, lies at the root of this is the status of the body as an essential part of the human person: "Is the body part of the true self? Do mystical experiences occur in the body or lead the spiritual quest irrevocably to an abandonment of all corporeality?"[48]

Here, the Platonic tradition, with its focus on the spirit as the most essential part of man, stood diametrically opposed to the beliefs within ancient Jewish tradition. In the latter tradition—and this is also in line with Chinese thinking—the body is an essential aspect of being human and not the breeding ground for all the evil that occurs in human existence. According to Paul Evdokimov, the opposite is rather the case: "evil does not come from below, from the physical, but from above, from the spiritual."[49]

In addition to the anthropological question about the status of the body of the human being, a fundamental theological question also arose, namely: Is it possible in this earthly body and with the physical senses of this body to perceive and to experience the Tabor light—the light that is in fact God? Or is God so fundamentally 'other than' and so elevated above physical, earthly reality that God is entirely unknowable and cannot possibly be experienced by any human being who is an entity of mind, soul *and* body?

From a radical, dualistic view of Reality, it is impossible to experience God in this earthly body and through its bodily senses. Over and over again the Churches of the East and the West were challenged to respond to this dualistic thinking. Throughout the centuries this has proved to be the grindstone on which 'orthodox' Christian thinking has had to sharpen and purify itself. It would, therefore, seem that the struggle which existential phenomenology fought against Cartesian dualism is part of a long tradition and has ancient roots.

---

introduced these thoughts into early Christianity. In gnostic thinking it was assumed that knowledge of the true self also entailed knowledge of the cosmos and even of God.
This self-knowledge was only reserved for a spiritual elite. The mediation of a church was not necessary to arrive at this knowledge of the Self and God. Most Christian Gnostic movements also had a strong dualistic approach whereby the earthly reality, including that of the human body, was seen as fundamentally bad.

[48] Andreopoulos, 218: *Is the body part of the true self? Are mystical experiences taking place in the body or is the spiritual quest destined to lead to abandonment or all corporeality?*

[49] Evdokimov, 63: *le mal ne vient pas d'en bas, du corporel, mais d'en haut du spirituel.*

The fundamental theological and anthropological questions regarding the experience of the Tabor light in the space of the body, led in the fourteenth century to a dramatic conflict within Eastern Orthodox Christianity. The reason we will now look at this struggle is because it relates to the existence of a transcendent dimension, present in our daily reality and to the value that our patients placed on transcendent experiences.

The aforementioned conflict erupted in full when Barlaäm of Calabria (1290–1348)[50] launched a frontal attack on the hesychastic methods of prayer and the theological notions which formed their foundations. Barlaäm was familiar with these because he had spent some time living in a monastery with monks who practiced such methods. Barlaäm ridiculed these practices and mockingly called the monks *omphaloskopoi,* navel gazers.

He accused the hesychasts of spiritual pride because they claimed to be able to see God with the eyes of their earthly bodies.[51] He argued that our human capacity of cognition is ultimately inadequate for knowing Reality-as-it-is. And this is certainly true for the Reality that is God.

According to Barlaäm, God is ultimately unknowable and God's light—just like the Tabor light—cannot be seen or experienced by a human being. Every assertion of such an experience is based on self-suggestion or is, according to him, the result of an 'atmospheric disturbance' at the most. In the separation that Barlaäm thus assumed between the Reality of God and that of humankind, it is clear that fundamental patterns of dualism can be recognised throughout the centuries.

Gregory Palamas (1296–1359) was a hesychastic teacher who lived for a long time in one of the monasteries on Mount Athos. It was especially with the

---

[50] Barlaäm of Calabria was a humanist philosopher, philologist and theologian from southern Italy and was trained in Aristotelian scholastics. The term 'umbilical starers' (*omphaloskopoi*), with which he ridiculed the hesychasts, comes from him. His doctrine was eventually rejected by three orthodox synods (the two 'councils of Sophia' in 1341 and the council of Blachernae in 1351). The teaching of his opponent Palamas has since been definitively embraced as the Orthodox.

[51] Bastiaansen, L. (1984) *De Thaborikoon: Theologie en Symboliek van de Ikonen* (The Tabor Icon: Theology and symbolism of icons), Zundert: Abbey Maria Toevlucht, 39.

monks of Mount Athos that hesychastic prayer practice flourished.[52] When Barlaäm unleashed his attack on the hesychastic practices, Palamas was asked to lead the fight that had stirred up such great turmoil in the Christian East.

The question which burned at the heart of this battle was whether or not people could truly and even physically experience the light which Christ radiated at the time of his transfiguration. Was the Tabor light, that the monks on Mount Athos were said to perceive, actually real or was it a figment of their imagination?

Within his theology, Palamas elaborated on a classic theme within Eastern Orthodox Christianity, namely the difference that exists between the essence of God (οὐσία) and the energies which emanate from God (the ἐνέργειαι θεοῦ, *energeiai theou*). He provided a theological underpinning to the idea that God exists in two modalities of being. In the depths of his being, God is totally transcendent, unknowable and cannot be perceived (Barlaäm would agree with this!), but is immanent in God's energies, meaning that divinity is present in all things and all living beings.

This means that, although God is ultimately unknowable in his innermost being, he can be experienced by human beings in and through his energies. This paradoxical way of thinking about the two modalities in which God exists was for Palamas the ultimate criterion for the correctness of the doctrine, that is to say for real 'orthodoxy'. The standpoint of Gregorius Palamas would become the official doctrine of the Eastern Orthodox Church during the Byzantine councils of the fourteenth century.

For Eastern Orthodox Christianity, the Tabor light represented the energetic and physically perceptible manifestation of God par excellence. It could actually be experienced by people who were willing to open themselves to this.

For the monks on Mount Athos, herein lay the theological justification for their efforts to discover the Tabor light within themselves and to experience God Himself in mind, soul *and* body. The theology of Gregorius Palamas challenged those streams of dualistic thinking which had existed from the earliest days of Christianity and which continued to surface in subsequent centuries. The conflict

---

[52] Mount Athos is a peninsula in northeastern Greece. A continuous monastic tradition has been present there since the ninth century. At the moment there are still approximately two thousand monks there, drawn from different countries of Eastern Orthodox Christianity.

in the fourteenth century was about the reality of transcendent experiences in and through the body.

The burning topic which raged all those centuries ago relates directly to the strange and 'unusual' experiences of our patients in the twenty-first century. Are they real or imaginary? Do they come from a healthy mind or, as some sceptics argue, from a mind poisoned by chemotherapy or some other medicine? Ultimately, what concerns us here is the precarious relationship between the body and spirituality.

The Tabor light: a real experience of God's energies?

The concept of *energeiai theou* as God's energetically outflowing presence in life itself is typical of Eastern Orthodox Christianity. In this, Eastern Orthodox Christianity distinguishes itself from Western Roman Christianity, as a result of which the separation that had already split Christianity in 1054 deepened even further. The Eastern Orthodox Churches increasingly focused on experiencing the inner Tabor light as the manifestation of the *energeiai theou* while the Western Church increasingly placed the emphasis on doctrine and morality.

The Church of Rome has never accepted Palamas' distinction between the essence of God and God's energies. It held fast to the 'simple' essence of God, in which there is no distinction between the unknowable, 'essence' of God which cannot be experienced and God's outflowing energies that are knowable and perceptible.

This means that if God is light, this light cannot be experienced by human beings. The theological view of the Church of Rome "allows for no other mode of existence for the deity than that of 'essence'. God is the 'Essential'. God's essence is 'Being'. What is not the 'Essence' does not belong to God and is not God."[53] This is why the experience of the Tabor light which was sought by the Eastern monks cannot be accepted by the Western Church as an experience of God.

---

[53] Bastiaansen, 30.

The body as an icon
Transparent membrane between two dimensions of reality

The position of the Eastern Orthodox Church, with regard to the body and the experience of God's *energeiai* in and through the body, can be better understood when viewed in the historical perspective of the victory over the 'iconoclastic controversy'.[54]

In the eighth century, a fierce battle raged within the Eastern Orthodox Church as to whether it was permissible to make images (icons) of Christ and the saints. Icons were destroyed on a large scale by the iconoclasts. To justify their actions they referred to a text in the Bible where it is stated clearly: "You shall not make for yourself an image in the form of anything in heaven above or on the earth beneath or in the waters below" (Ex.20:4).

In the religiously held conviction of the iconoclasts, the immeasurable distance between God and humankind, between spirit and body had to be respected. According to them, images of God and the saints were a denigration of the sacred and were seen as a form of idolatry in which a material image was regarded as equal to a spiritual reality.[55]

In fact, in this iconoclasm the separation between spirit and matter, mind and body so characteristic of Neo-Platonism, also manifested itself in the early days of the eighth century. In this split, the spirit was always seen as intrinsically good, with matter—and therefore every image made of matter—being intrinsically bad and an obstacle to reaching the spirit.[56] Although the Council of Chalcedon had already spoken strongly against these dualistic ideas in 451, they persistently

---

[54] Iconoclasm: The iconoclastic period, during which the making and worshiping of icons was forbidden, was inaugurated when the Byzantine Emperor Leo III had the famous icon of Christ removed from above the upper gate to the palace in Constantinople. In 730, he banned all icon worship in an edict. It was only during the reign of Empress Theodora that icon worship was restored in 843. Icons could once again be 'honored', but not worshiped. To the present day, on the first Sunday of Lent, the Eastern Churches celebrate the rehabilitation of the icon as the 'Triumph of Orthodoxy'.

[55] Evdokimov, P. (1970) *L'art de L'Icône, Théologie de la beauté*, Bruges, Paris: Desclée De Brouwer, 167.

[56] Ouspensky, L. (1922) *Theology of the Icon,* Volume 1, Crestwood, NY: St. Vladimir's Seminary Press, 148.

returned in ever new forms during the following centuries. The iconoclastic storm that raged in the Byzantine East was one such moment.

The ultimate argument that was brought into this theological dispute by Eastern Orthodox theologians to rein in the criticism of the iconoclasts and to neutralise the seemingly crucial text of Exodus 20:4 was the reality of the Incarnation. By becoming a man of flesh and blood, Jesus Christ had physically and materially fully descended into the matter of earthly reality. It was through his Incarnation that the immeasurable distance, which had always been assumed between 'above' and 'below', heaven and earth, God and humankind, was annihilated.

The improbable and incomprehensible 'descent' of the Divine into material reality is described in an exemplary way in Paul's Letter to the Philippians: "...who, though he was in the form of God, did not regard equality with God as something to be exploited, but emptied himself, taking the form of a slave, being born in human likeness. And being found in human form, he humbled himself[57] and became obedient to the point of death—even death on a cross." (Phil.2:6–8)[58]

It was thanks to the Incarnation of God in Jesus that physical, earthly reality would no longer be radically separated from God. The abolition of this separation through the Incarnation of God in Jesus Christ is the central theme of all 'orthodoxy', Eastern and Western.

This was to set up a barrier against all heresies, which allowed the separation between the divine and the earthly to persist and always absolutized one pole at the expense of the other. The essence of the orthodox doctrine is that in the person of Jesus Christ, the two contradictory realities of the human and the divine, as his two 'natures', are perfectly present and integrated. The doctrine of 'two natures in one person' was explicitly and definitively formulated as the fundamental truth of faith at the Council of Chalcedon in 451 CE.

The Orthodox Eastern Church has more radically considered the consequences of this than the Christian Western Church. The conclusion that was drawn here was: if God has 'humbled' himself by becoming a human being and by taking on a human body, then this implies that the physical reality of humankind is deified and thus 'raised' to God. This is called the *commercium*

---

[57] This refers to the crucial aspect of *kenosis*, self-emptying, i.e. Christ's taking on human existence.

[58] New Revised Standard Version.

admirabile, the miraculous exchange: God has become human so that the human can become God.[59]

This also rehabilitates the place of the body and, at the same time, that of the entire earthly, material reality. In their fight against the separation of body and mind, the existentialist phenomenologists have ancient comrades-in-arms on their side. In a culturally totally different context and in completely different terms, the same struggle was waged for the restoration of the human body and earthly reality.

That earthly reality is permeated with the divine also implies a substantial reassessment of the icon. As physical matter, an image on wood and made of paint, the icon is nonetheless permeated with the divine and has a transparent quality that offers a vision into divine reality. From the point of view of Eastern Orthodox Christianity, the icon is a transparent 'membrane' between two dimensions of reality, and not just a painting on a wooden board.

In hesychastic spirituality, this also applies to the human body. The body also carries within it the potential to be a transparent membrane for an underlying, all-permeating divine reality.

Incarnation, centring, transcendence within hesychasm

On the basis of the experiences of the patients which were described in Chapter Four, we have formulated the process involved in a lived and embodied spirituality in terms of *incarnation, centring* and *transcendence*. We have seen how centring appears to be the connecting link between incarnation and transcendence. By means of an analysis of the Tabor icon, it is possible to demonstrate how hesychasm gives substance to these three terms and how the contradiction, which is often assumed between incarnation and transcendence, is overcome.

At the beginning of this chapter, we said that we would take a closer look at the icon of the Transfiguration of Jesus Christ on Mount Tabor. We have printed the most famous picture of this icon which was painted by Theophanes the Greek[60] in the fifteenth century.

---

[59] The classical Greek term for human beings becoming God is *'theosis'*.

[60] Theophanes the Greek (1340–14_0) was born in the Byzantine Empire and worked in Constantinople. In 1370, he moved to Novgorod and later (1395) to Moscow. He was the teacher of Rublev who is considered the most important Russian icon painter.

Figure 2

And he was transfigured before them, and his face shone like the sun, and his clothes became dazzling white. (Matt. 17.2)[61]

---

[61] We quote here the New Revised Standard Version, 1989.

The icon depicts the far-reaching reality of the Incarnation, namely of God's humbling 'descent' into the flesh and blood of a human being: God being 'grounded' in the body of the man Jesus. In fact, Andreopoulos writes: "The Transfiguration of Jesus Christ is one of the most fascinating images of Christianity. Nothing can measure up to its extraordinary grandeur. It encompasses and unfolds the essence of the Christian faith."[62]

A second aspect of incarnation is expressed through the cross-shaped arrangement of the figures in the icon of the Transfiguration. Regarding this, various authors point to a form of the Cross with two cross beams, from the Russian Orthodox tradition (see fig. 1). Forming the horizontal beam are the figures of Moses, Elijah and Christ, whilst the three disciples—Peter, James and John—form the lower oblique beam.

With this particular cruciform pattern, the connection becomes visible between the glorification of Jesus Christ on Mount Tabor and his crucifixion on the Mount of Golgotha. It is not without reason, therefore, that the moment of transfiguration is described in the gospels of Matthew, Mark and Luke directly after Jesus has first spoken plainly of his suffering and death. Here we see that transfiguration and crucifixion go together. These two key events, polarities, mark the highest and lowest moments of Jesus' earthly life. Together, they signify the ultimate nature of Christ's Incarnation.

Fig. 1   Fig.2   Fig. 3

A further aspect of incarnation can be illustrated through another form of cross: a more ancient cross with four arms of equal length (see fig. 2) which pre-

---

[62] Andreopoulos, 15.

dates the more familiar Latin Cross (see fig 3) from the time of Constantine the Great. The older, four-armed cross—which implies the shape of a square—is depicted in different spiritual traditions and religions. For example, this cross appears in Chinese Daoism as 'the symbol par excellence of the earth'.

Here the number four symbolises earthly reality and points to what is tangible and perceptible.[63] This gives incarnation in material reality a much wider scope. It does not only happen in the body of one human being, Jesus Christ, but also signifies a descent of the divine into the whole of the earthly realm.

Centring

In the four-armed cruciform shape (see fig. 2), the point of intersection of the horizontal and vertical beams is highly significant. According to De Roselyne, this midpoint is "the pre-eminent place of breakthrough at all levels, of all transitions, from one world to another." Following the famous philosopher of religion, Mircea Eliade, he writes that in the centre of the cross—and this is especially true for the cross on which Jesus Christ died—the distance that separates humankind from God is eradicated, once and for all.

In every icon of the Transfiguration, the critical point of intersection lies in the centre of Christ's body. This coincides remarkably with the centre of the mandorla, the radiant light which encircles him. This central crossing point is found by drawing a vertical and horizontal line through the mandorla.

What is striking here is that the light of the mandorla does not emanate from the heart or head of the Christ figure, but from the centre of his lower body. This precise, central point of intersection is therefore no mere artistic coincidence. Instead, it points to an essential Christological and theological significance. In the icon of the Transfiguration, the centre of the body and the mandorla is the connecting point between two dimensions that were previously thought to be radically separate, namely the human and the divine.

A recurring motif, visible on most icons of the Transfiguration, is the light that emanates in all directions from the centre of the figure of Jesus Christ. This light symbolises the breakthrough of the divine through Christ's physical form. That is why, before starting, an icon painter draws a big eye in the middle of the empty surface on which the icon is to be painted. This symbolises the eye of

---

[63] de Roselyne, F. (1978) 'L'Icône de la Transfiguration', *Spiritualité Orientale et Vie Monastique, no.23*, Bégrolles en Mauges: Abbaye de Bellefontaine, 91.

God, the invisible centre of the entire image, the source of all rays of light. From this eye, the entire figure of Christ is irradiated and the space around him illuminated. Often, in icons of the Transfiguration, this light is represented as an oval-shaped mandorla.

However, occasionally sometimes it is shown as three concentric circles which darken in proximity to the centre, as in the icon of Theophanes. The darkness symbolises the aspect of the Godhead which is beyond all human understanding.

Often pointed out is a strong similarity between the mandorla, in Christian iconography and the mandala, from Hindu and Tibetan Buddhist iconography.[64] The mandala is a schematic representation of cosmic reality in which a circle, as a symbol of eternity (heaven), contains a square, symbolising finiteness and all corporeality (earth).

In the centre of the mandala—which in Hindu and Tibetan Buddhist traditions represents a map of the cosmos—the highest deity (for example Shiva or the Buddha) is depicted and seen as the source of transcendent light. In psychological terms, this can be considered as the innermost light, *the shining aspect of consciousness.* There are, therefore, interesting similarities between the mandala of Eastern spirituality and the mandorla of Christian iconography.

In the Christian mandorla, which can also be viewed as a mandala, Jesus Christ stands as the light-radiating centre of all created reality. It is through this emanating light that reality is transformed into a 'mirror without blemish'.[65] Christ, in the Tabor icon, represents the ideal image of deified humankind.

The 'Jesus Prayer', originating from the Orthodox tradition, leads into the heart, the centre of the mandorla, and into union with God. The reciting of the prayer also involves becoming centred in one's own body. It is not about following Christ but becoming Christ, literally and physically. This centripetal movement towards the centre is something that we will revisit in the final chapter of this book. It is a movement that represents the crucial dynamic which lies at the very heart of our vision of a lived and embodied spirituality.

---

[64] A mandala is a schematic representation of cosmic reality, in which within a circle as a symbol of the infinite (heaven) a square is drawn as a symbol of the finite (the earth). According to C.G. Jung the mandala was a symbol for psychic integration.
[65] Andreopoulos, 233.

As a first example of transcendence, the 'admirabele commercium', which we wrote about earlier, can be mentioned: God becomes a human being so that human beings can become God.[66] A gap that was once deemed irreconcilable has been transcended from two directions. From God, the gap is transcended from above to below; from humankind, the gap is transcended from below to above.

It is also here that the 'breakthrough' from one level to another comes to the fore, which an author such as De Roselyne writes about repeatedly. Hesychasm offers techniques of prayer and meditation so that the human level can be transcended and a person becomes open to the descent of the divine light. This is the *theosis*, becoming God that would become the central theme within Eastern Orthodox spirituality. This also encapsulates the ambition to definitively overcome the duality between mind and body, God and humankind.

Another moment of transcendence involves the actual space that is represented by the mandorla. The mandorla is the light which emanates from and surrounds the figure of Christ on the Tabor icon. In its circumference, this circle of light extends beyond the Christ figure and illuminates a space that is essentially limitless and encompasses the entire world, the cosmos and all people.

When the Tabor icon is also viewed as a mandala with the supreme deity at its very heart, in this case Jesus Christ, then the universal, all-embracing symbolism of it is unmistakable. Maximos the Confessor, one of the Church Fathers, wrote, as early as the seventh century, that the countless individualities of the members of the Church—with the *myriads of differences among them*—are connected through Christ as the centre of the circle *as by one heart and mind.*

Finally, a transcendent moment can also be identified in the icon itself. It is not just a painting on a board of wood but a transparent membrane between earthly and divine reality. The icon therefore also has a 'reversed perspective', which means that the viewer not only looks at an icon, but is also viewed from a space on the other side of the icon.

Therefore, with this in mind, looking at an icon is in itself an act of transcendence. The crucial point is to be able to look through the icon and to be

---

[66] Also within Western Christianity has someone like Meister Eckhart described this theme of a human being becoming God in relation to the Incarnation of God, i.e. God becoming a human being.

open to another reality that lights up and permeates the whole of the icon. In the icon itself, the separation between material and spiritual reality is thus transcended and abolished.

Experiencing the transcendent Tabor light is the basic motive of hesychasm. The prayer life of the hermits in the desert and of the monks in their monasteries was focused on experiencing this 'un-created' divine light.[67] However, this experience was not reserved for monks in the remote places of monasteries or deserts.

For example, it was assumed that icon painters themselves also had to be illuminated by the same light that Christ radiated on Mount Tabor. Painting the Tabor icon was therefore proof of having mastered this art form. The painting of icons was viewed as a mystical art, because in experiencing the Tabor light, the icon painter was thought to be permeated by the *energeiai* of God.

Therefore, in the process of painting the icon, a transcendent reality is incarnated into a practical skill. This would only be possible if the painter had inwardly experienced the Tabor light and therefore did not simply paint with colours derived from earthly reality but also with 'light'. It is not only icon painters but also patients with cancer who are sometimes able to catch a glimpse and sometimes more than that, of a light that comes from within.

Integration of incarnation, centring and transcendence

The two natures: the Council of Chalcedon:

In the icon of the Transfiguration on Mount Tabor, the Orthodox East sought to show the ultimate unification of God and humankind. It is a unification that comes together in Jesus Christ. He is incarnated in the flesh of a human body and, at the same time, is also transcendent in his divinity. Both of these dimensions permeate each other in the radiant centre of his being, as concretely visualised on the Tabor icon.

According to orthodox theologians, the human and divine dimensions of existence, which were previously deemed to be absolute opposites, are unified in Christ, in the moment of transfiguration on Mount Tabor.

---

[67] The mystical significance of light was practically kept secret within the ascetic tradition until the tenth century when Simeon the New Theologian first spoke openly about his ecstatic experiences of the divine light (Andreopoulos, 185).

This unlikely and incomprehensible combination of these two opposite realities was the central theme of the Council of Chalcedon. This was formulated in the confession of the two natures which are united in the one person of Jesus Christ:

"Following the example of the holy fathers, we all unanimously confess that our Lord Jesus Christ is to us one and the same Son, perfect in his Deity and perfect in his Humanity, truly God and truly Man—the Only Begotten Son of God, in two natures, unmixed, unchanged, undivided, unseparated; in addition, the distinction between the natures is in no way nullified by the union, but rather the characteristic features of each nature being preserved and brought together in one person and one hypostasis …"

For the first time, the words 'hypostasis' and 'person' were used in an ecclesiastical document of vital importance, to indicate the intrinsic unity of two radically different natures in the one person of Jesus Christ. The doctrine, that in the person of Jesus Christ two natures are united, applies in Eastern Orthodox theology in principle to the 'personhood' of all people!

In the *commercium admirabile*, divine reality has become so deeply connected to human reality that this has become essentially joined to divine reality and is completely permeated by it. This means that all Christology is at the same time anthropology. The well-known Orthodox theologian Kallistos Ware calls this the polestar of all Orthodox-Christian anthropology.[68]

Two natures, one person: the structure of the Tabor icon

The merging of opposite poles is clearly reflected in the way that the Tabor icon often uses the circle and the square (both of which lie at the heart of the mandala) as two basic patterns that together must form a unity. This points to nothing less than the human and the divine co-existing and being intrinsically united with each other.

Interestingly, Theophanes the Greek did not paint a square and circle in his icon of the Transfiguration, but two luminous triangles which overlap each other, in and around a centre. One triangle is 'descending' and symbolises the divine

---

[68] Ware, K. and Chirban, J. (Ed) (1996) 'In the Image and Likeness. The Uniqueness of the Human Person', *Personhood—Orthodox Christianity and the Connection Between Body, Mind and Soul,* Westport: Bergin & Garvey, 2.

nature directed towards human and earthly reality: the other is 'ascending' and symbolises the nature of humankind and the world striving for divine reality.

The theologian Andreopoulos, just like C.G Jung, sees a 'yantra' in these two interpenetrating triangles. This is a variant of the mandala pattern which is frequently used in Tibet and India to express the unity of two counterparts in a centre. In Hinduism, this centre symbolises the oneness of Shiva and Shakti, the divine-masculine and the divine-feminine, which, like the Yin and Yang in Chinese Daoism, are the expression of an underlying unity.

Centring in the mandala: the way to personhood

According to C.G Jung, the yantra expresses the unity of the 'personal, time bound world of the ego with a non-personal, timeless world of the non-ego or the union of the soul with God'. Therefore, the yantra corresponds very closely to the pattern and the religious content of the icon of the Transfiguration, which points to the unity of human and divine natures in the one person, Jesus Christ.

Where the icon of the Transfiguration seeks to express a theological reality, Jung sees in this a psychological reality and interprets the two mutually interpenetrating triangles of the yantra as a symbol of the process of individuation, of 'the healing of the psyche or the Self', in which the unconscious is integrated into the conscious. Patients speak about this at the end of their process in a simpler way: "Now, at last, I am the person who I really am."

Although individuation, as the integration of opposites, is a concept from twentieth century psychology, it definitely has a clear connection with fundamental theological, Christological and anthropological themes in the history of Eastern Orthodox Christianity. It is a continuation of the theme of 'becoming a person' in the merging of two apparently opposite dimensions of reality: the human and the divine, the finite and infinite.

Limitations of the perspective of hesychasm

As with the Qi Gong practice, hesychasm offers a window for viewing the more 'unusual', transcendent experiences of the patients. However, it should not be forgotten that there are also major differences. For example, the experiences of patients with regard to the loss of future, meaning in life and the accompanying fear of death do not occur in the hesychastic literature.

The path to transcendent experiences is a very different one for cancer patients than it is for the monks who practiced hesychasm. A monk goes into the desert to lead a self-chosen lonely and ascetic life. Our patients enter the hospital and undergo an 'asceticism' they did not ask for, in the form of side effects from major medical treatments. Both situations are very extreme and induce a profound change in the way of living: in the view of Reality and in the experience of the Self.

The solitude that a monk seeks in the desert to find God is a different experience to the loneliness of patients who feel excluded from work, family life and social companionship. As a result, they are, against their will, thrown back on themselves. Whilst the practitioners of hesychasm could still remain within the meaning-giving system of their culture and beliefs, cancer patients fall outside of the familiar framework of the meaning-giving system of Western culture.

The experience of one's own finitude and being incarnated in a mortal body is also very different. Whereas practitioners of hesychasm have a firm faith in the continuation of life after death, such trust is no longer there in Western culture. The confrontation with death faced by cancer patients is therefore often more penetrating and frightening. The fact that experiences of transcendence nevertheless occur in a number of patients is a real paradox.

Considering these differences between the hesychastic world and that of cancer patients, there are also remarkable similarities in the experience of the body. We will discuss this further in the next chapter.

Overview of the central concepts in Qi Gong and hesychasm

Shown below is a summary of the most important shifts (shown by the arrows) within Qi Gong and hesychasm in terms of the concepts of incarnation, centring and transcendence. In addition, the table contains a column headed 'integration' which summarises how the three concepts of incarnation, centring and transcendence come together within the perspective of these two traditions. At a glance, the summary attempts to show parallels between the two traditions and how they use different language and accentuate different experiences.

Qi Gong				
	The connection between body and mind is self-evident.	Making a stronger connection in the centre of the body, becoming anchored in it.	An inner movement of energy from Dantian to the heart and head.	Centring, connecting incarnation and transcendence.
	Deeper relaxation results In a stronger flow of energy (Qi).	Breathing from the body's centre results in increased vitality.	An outer movement of energy connecting with the Great One.	Embracing, Yin and Yang, the paradox of polarity.
	Balancing fire Qi and water Qi promotes physical and mental health.	Balancing the Yang and Yin creates connection with Dantian, lower abdomen.	Creating a circulating cycle of light within the body.	Becoming a True Human Being (zhen ren), integrating the individual with Cosmic reality.

Hesychasm	Overcoming the body-mind separation through Incarnation.	Focusing on the body's centre, inspired by the icon's mandorla.	Descending (God into a human being); ascending (a human being into God).	Centring, connecting incarnation and transcendence.
	Hesychia, creating inner tranquillity to experience God's presence.	Centring, opening to a space beyond thought and emotions.	Experiencing unity with God as inner light: Tabor light.	Divine and human nature are integrated in the centre, becoming a Person.
	Becoming free of passions, creating a balance of mind.	Trans-centring, as breaking through from one dimension to another.	Transcending the centre: uniting with God, connecting with the cosmos.	Becoming a Person, living the paradox of the two realities: Imitatio Christi.

Part Three:
Towards a Vision of a Lived and Embodied Spirituality

Chapter Eight
Experiences of the Patients Viewed from the Perspectives of Existential Phenomenology, Qi Gong and Hesychasm

Introduction

What does the journey into the perspectives of existential phenomenology, Qi Gong and hesychasm bring? To what extent do they help us to understand the experiences of our patients in coping with a life-threatening disease? Do they offer deeper insight into what lived and embodied spirituality is?

We decided to draw on these philosophical-spiritual traditions because they provide a more encompassing and a cross-cultural framework for interpreting and valuing the experiences of the patients at a deeper level.

Furthermore, these experiences, viewed through the lenses of these three perspectives, might also turn out to be relevant to other people.

The three perspectives offer different windows for looking at what it means to live with a life-threatening illness.

- Through the window of existential phenomenology, we can view the 'horizontal-immanent dimension', where the finiteness of life comes to the fore in the inexorable confrontation with death. This awareness of mortality eventually forces itself upon everyone, whether sick or healthy.
- Through the window of Qi Gong, we can look at the 'vertical transcendent dimension' where people experience themselves as part of a greater whole—of nature and the cosmos and as a natural unity of body, soul and spirit.

- Through the window of hesychasm we can simultaneously behold the horizontal-immanent and vertical-transcendent dimensions—the 'finite and the infinite', the mortal and immortal, the 'human and the divine'. It is in realising the inherent unity of these antipoles that a human being becomes the person who he or she essentially is.

The three windows offer a way of exploring both the horizontal-immanent and vertical-transcendent dimensions of the patients' experiences. Both of these are needed in order to do justice to their experiences. We will now look again at these two dimensions by briefly revisiting the concepts of *incarnation, centring* and *transcendence,* as they figure within the three perspectives and relate them more explicitly to the patients' experiences.

Relevance of existential phenomenology to the concepts of incarnation, centring and transcendence

Incarnation within existential phenomenology

In the Western world, our awareness of mortality tends to be repressed through the many feverish activities which characterise daily life. According to Heidegger, we are not the autonomous subjects of our actions, but are the objects and victims of our fears, of others' expectations and of many social conventions.

We focus our attention on the outside world and strive to achieve goals for a sometimes distant future, leaving little energy for living life in the here and now and truly experiencing our bodies. It is only when a life-threatening illness strikes that we become aware of the finite nature of life and the vulnerability of our body. This is something that we saw so clearly in the lives of our patients. Heidegger's conclusion is that most people today avoid facing the truth that they are physically incarnated, mortal beings. He calls this a state of 'decay' (German: *Verfallenheit*).

This sobering analysis provided by an existential phenomenology of the current 'condition humaine' resonates with our description of the patients' experience of their body before they fell ill, when the so-called functional-instrumental had precedence over the sensory-sensitive experience of the body. Heidegger's words open up a dramatically deeper layer and offer a clear connection between a particular experience of the body with a certain 'view of Reality' and 'experience of the Self'.

Centring in existential phenomenology

The concept of centring has a different content in existential phenomenology than in Qi Gong and hesychasm. It has a definite psychological significance and stands for 'becoming a subject' in the confrontation with death and in daring to realise our mortality. For Heidegger, the confrontation with our mortality is a 'wake-up call'. It awakens us from the illusory and bland existence in which death is cowardly banished from consciousness.

According to him, this existential shock offers the ultimate opportunity for us to 'centre' ourselves, to become an autonomous subject, i.e. a real *I-self*. For a number of our patients, the diagnosis of a life-threatening disease instigated such a 'wake-up call'. They were thrown back on themselves and had to become, whether they liked it or not, a somebody: a subject, different from many others.

Becoming a subject is, in our thinking, an important aspect of a lived and embodied spirituality, although this is often not recognised as such. More often, it is emphasised that spirituality is about getting rid of the 'I', the 'ego'. Nonetheless, for a cancer patient, the process of becoming an *I-self* is a vital step in coping with the disease, dealing with the medical system and giving personal meaning to the quality of his or her life.

Transcendence in existential phenomenology

In addition to the above, the interpretation given by existential phenomenology to the concept of transcendence is also very different from that of Qi Gong and hesychasm. In existential phenomenology, transcendence stays within the horizontal-immanent perspective of Reality. It concerns the relationships that people have with the concrete reality of things and the people around them.

It would be wrong to underestimate the value of this horizontal-immanent form of transcendence. In the concrete reality of their lives, it is more important than ever for patients to be able to relate and respond adequately to the specific situations they encounter. Because of a diminished physical condition and loss of vitality and energy, they simply cannot live in the same way as they did before their illness.

In relating to others, they now have to make choices and set limits to what is expected of them and what they expect of themselves. It is inevitable, even necessary, that they become more aware of their needs, limitations and priorities and communicate these effectively to others. This is a form of transcendence that does not rise 'upwards', but goes 'forwards' and takes place in the concrete social, horizontal-immanent field of life. This kind of transcendence significantly contributes to the quality of life that must be fought for under extremely difficult circumstances.

Relevance of Qi Gong and hesychasm to the concepts of incarnation, centring and transcendence

Incarnation in Qi Gong and hesychasm

- *Beyond the separation of body and mind*

It is clear from our earlier descriptions of both traditions that the relationship between body and mind is fundamental, particularly with regard to psycho-spiritual and religious development. In Chinese culture, the unity of body and mind has always been self-evident and a dualistic view of the world and humankind has therefore never developed.

Hesychasm, on the other hand, originated in a culture in which a strong dualism determined the image of human beings and a positive relationship between body and mind was not self-evident. Yet, in hesychasm this dualism was radically broken through. Hesychasm based itself—following the first Church Fathers and the Council of Chalcedon—on the crucial fact of the Incarnation of Jesus Christ in flesh and blood. His Incarnation meant recognising and fully accepting the physical aspect of human life and the suffering and death which are an essential part of this.

In the chapter on hesychasm, we have seen that this Incarnation meant not only acknowledging and even elevating the human body but also embracing the whole earth and the entirety of material reality.

When patients are diagnosed with cancer, the relationship between body and mind is no longer self-evident. Patients often speak of feeling betrayed and abandoned by their bodies. The treatments for their illness and the consequences thereof (amputation, hair loss, energy loss, etc.) are so radical that many patients feel deeply alienated from their own body. The body is no longer the willing instrument through which they can realise their goals and ambitions.

Yet, in coping with the disease and regaining a quality of life, it becomes clear that the restoration of the relationship between body and mind is of utmost importance. For patients, it is necessary that this separation between body and mind is overcome, not in an intellectual but in a truly experiential way.

- *Experience of the flow of energy*

Remarkably, in Qi Gong and hesychasm the reality of the 'spiritual' is experienced as a flow of energies. The way in which these energies are described within the two traditions is different. In Qi Gong, these energies are called Qi and are an impersonal, cosmic, vital life-force. In hesychasm, these energies are called the *energeiai theou* and are considered to emanate from God himself.

Despite these different wordings and interpretations—non-theistic and theistic—there is common ground which revolves around the actual experience of energies in the body. In both traditions, being incarnated in the body involves a conscious and physical experience of these energies.

This flow of energy corresponds to the experiences of some patients during the psycho-energetic exercises and the haptonomic massages. When they talk about this, they hesitantly search for the words to describe this flowing energy in their body, something which they had never experienced before. They articulate this movement in a very personal way, often drawing on images and metaphors.

For some, these energies come from the natural environment: the earth beneath, heaven above, the cosmos all around. Others interpret these energies in a religious way as an experience of the divine, God or the love of Jesus.

When counselling patients, it is important to give them space and time to find the words and concepts that are most meaningful to them. When sensing this flow of energies, the connection between mind and body is present in a deeply experiential way. It can bring comfort and encouragement, often reducing anxiety and fear, even the fear of death.

- *Receptivity as a condition for experiencing flowing energy*

In order to experience this flowing energy, it is important to relax deeply (Qi Gong) and to find inner peace of mind (hesychasm). The turmoil of the mind and the restless emotions which this brings about needs to be brought to a place of rest.

In Qi Gong, this is done by establishing a balance between 'fire Qi' and 'water Qi'; in hesychasm, by overcoming the passions of the heart and emptying the mind. Experiencing this flowing energy is not achieved through an act of will (willpower). It is arrived at through a state of openness, by not 'doing' (the so-called *Wu Wei* in Qi Gong) or by being receptive to divine grace (hesychasm). The necessity of being receptive to this kind of experience presupposes that it comes from a different dimension (nature, the cosmos or God) and cannot be a fabricated psychic projection.

Patients need to experience relaxation and deep rest as the first step in breaking free from 'the merry-go-round of thinking' and the multitude of feelings and emotions which this evokes. It is only at this point that the flowing energy can be experienced. This usually seems to happen spontaneously, independent of will and/or desire. It marks a shift from the functional-instrumental body experience to that of the sensory-sensitive (see Chapter Three), of which the latter represents a deeper form of being incarnated.

Centring in Qi Gong and hesychasm

- *The importance of the body's centre*

In both traditions, great importance is attached to experience contact with the centre of the body. In Qi Gong, this is the Dantian. It is the place in the body where the energies from earth and heaven are absorbed and concentrated and thus experienced as a source of vitality and inner strength.

In the icon of the Transfiguration, the centre of Jesus Christ's body is clearly indicated in the lower space of his pelvis. It is even depicted at a lower level than that of the Dantian in Qi Gong.

The centre that is indicated in the icon of the Transfiguration corresponds to the breathing centre which the patients speak about when doing psycho-energetic bodywork. This centre also has a lower position than that of the Dantian within

Qi Gong practice and is located in a space directly in front of the sacrum.[69] It matches precisely with the middle that is seen in the icon of the Transfiguration.[70]

Patients say that when they are in contact with this centre, they are actually more in their body and experience it more fully and describe a feeling of being more in contact with themselves. Remarkably, they often say that in the act of breathing in and through this centre, they experience a different 'state of being'—beyond their pain, fatigue and emotions.

- *Going through the centre*

In the traditions of Qi Gong and hesychasm, contact with this centre has even more significance. The centre of the body is the passage to another, more transcendent dimension. In Qi Gong, this presents a gateway to cosmic reality and opens the way for experiencing the Dao, through which 'the Great One' can be realised. In hesychasm, the body's centre represents the gateway to God. It signifies a *rupture of level* which opens up the possibility of reciprocal action between human beings and God.

When patients are connected with the centre of their body, they not only speak about being more in contact with themselves, but of having an experience of 'space', 'energy' and 'light'. Their words indicate that in and beyond this centre another dimension of reality opens up.

Transcendence in Qi Gong and hesychasm

- *Realising oneself as part of a larger whole: the cosmos, God*

In both of these traditions, being anchored in the centre of the body creates an openness to 'a larger whole'. In this state of openness, according to Qi Gong, practitioners find themselves in the midst of earth and heaven. Like a microcosm,

---

[69] The location of this centre is clearly indicated in the various books by Hetty Draayer. See: Draayer, H. (2007) *Finde Dich Selbst durch Meditation,* (Darmstadt: Schirner Verlag. Idem (2010) *Meditatie, energie en bewustzijn: De Innerlijke weg vanuit het kosmisch oog,* 2nd edition, Rotterdam, De Driehoek.

[70] This agreement only emerged during our study of hesychasm. Initially this had not been recognized.

they reflect the macrocosm and are, in every fibre of their body, connected with it.

Reflecting the figure of Christ, practitioners of hesychasm experience—from the centre of the body—a space that extends far beyond the circumference of the body.

It is clear that in both traditions, transcendence coincides with being deeply centred and therefore incarnated in the body.

The theme of transcendence, as it appears in the two traditions, provides a framework for the experiences of transcendence, about which patients speak. They often say that they feel part of 'a larger whole'. Some even talk about the skin becoming transparent, where the boundary which the skin is often seen to represent, dissolves.

Incarnation, centring and transcendence: integration

Incarnation, centring and *transcendence* interweave and form a trinity. Centring takes central stage and connects the apparently opposite poles of incarnation and transcendence. In this, the traditions of Qi Gong and hesychasm correspond to each other.

Centred in the body, a human being is incarnated in the concrete physical corporeality and from that bodily centre transcends the boundaries of the visual shape of the body and is connected to the space around. When the immanent and the transcendent dimensions of being come together, Qi Gong then speaks of the True Human Being (*zhen ren*). Hesychasm speaks of God-Wo(man), a 'person' existing in two natures.

The terminology of these spiritual traditions seems to be far removed from the language and world of experience of current daily life. That is why it is all the more remarkable that several patients speak about the experience of being 'in two dimensions': finite and infinite, mortal and immortal. At the same time, they say they are 'more themselves than ever' or that it is 'only now that they are truly themselves'. In the final chapter, becoming who one truly is returns as the core theme of our vision of a lived and embodied spirituality.

Overview of central concepts

Upwards directed arrows: tendency is dominant
Downwards directed arrows: tendency is subdominant
Horizontal arrows: indicates a balance.

	Stage 1 before illness	Stage 2 at diagnosis	Stage 3 during treatment	Stage 4 after five years
Bodily experiences of the patients: functional-instrumental (FI) and sensory-sensitive (SS).	**FI ↑ SS ↓** No awareness of finitude	**FI ↓ SS ↓** Awareness of finitude	**FI ↓ SS ↑** Suffering from side effects of treatment.	**FI ↔ SS** Balance in functional-instrumental and sensory-sensitive bodily awareness.
	(all groups)	(all groups)	(all groups) Experiences that transcend suffering (groups 1 and 2)	(all groups)
Existential phenomenology	Repressing fear of death *incarnation↓* *centring ↓* *transcendence ↓*	Confrontation with the fear of death *Incarnation ↑* *centring as subject ↑* *transcendence ↑*		Facing death and enduring the fear of it.
	Living as *one of them*	**Living as** *I-self* **Horizontal immanent dimension of meaning**		**Living as** *a subject* **in the world**
	(all groups)	(all groups)		(all groups)

Qi Gong & Hesychasm	Finiteness is no theme	Finiteness and fear of death are no themes	Suffering has a place **Centring in the body centre** *Incarnation↑ centring and ↑ transcendence ↑* **Vertical-transcendent dimension of meaning:** human being ↔ cosmos; human being ↔ god	**Integrating opposites:** finite (human being) ↔ infinite (cosmos). **Living as a 'True human being'** (Qi Gong) finite (human being) ↔ infinite (god). **Living as a 'Person'** (hesychasm)
	(not applicable to our groups)	(not applicable to our groups)	(groups 1 and 2)	becoming who you really are (groups 1 and 2)

Chapter Nine
Centring and Trans-Centring: A-Body Oriented Vision of Lived Spirituality

Losing me, becoming me

"From the first chemo, it was disastrous. I was nauseous day and night ... I just wanted ... to die. My body became a living hell. This body—that I so desperately wanted to keep and love like nothing else, became my greatest enemy.

"I find it difficult to say what actually happened there. It was not something I saw with my eyes, but everything lit up. There was another light. There was a new glow ... everything was lit up differently. Everything."

Introduction: The struggle to find balance

In this chapter, we now interweave the many strands we have unfurled in the previous chapters to develop our vision of a lived and embodied spirituality. We see this as a process which is dialectic in character. In Chapter Two, we described how, in the course of four stages of their illness, cancer patients experienced their body and the often dramatic changes that come with it. We looked at how these changes impacted on their view of Reality and their sense of Self.

In Chapter Three, we looked at how patients described the changes in bodily awareness. It was here that we distinguished between a 'functional-instrumental' experience of the body and a 'sensory sensitive' one. In Chapter Four, we looked at the sometimes remarkable differences between the groups who had received counselling and psycho-energetic bodywork at Tabor House and the group who did not.

In trying to capture the essence of the experience of the body among the patients who had participated in psycho-energetic bodywork, three concepts came to the fore: *incarnation* (being in touch with the body), *centring* (being

129

connected with the centre within the body) and *transcendence* (being related to a larger whole). With these concepts in mind, we studied three philosophical-spiritual traditions: existential phenomenology, Qi Gong and hesychasm to see whether they would offer a broader perspective and a deeper understanding of the experiences of the patients.

We now bring all these strands together and present our vision of a lived and embodied spirituality. We do this under the headings of 'centring' and 'trans-centring'. These are key terms which are crucial in our vision of spirituality as a process with a centripetal, i.e. centre-directed dialectic. Using these terms, we are able to capture, interpret and value the many and very diverse experiences of the patients and understand them as particular moments in a spiritual process.

Of course, the patients themselves never used words like 'centring' and 'trans-centring'. For them, dealing with their illness involved an intense struggle to come to terms with what happened to them and their bodies. Feeling devastated and completely thrown off balance, they struggled to find a new balance at many levels of their existence. In our vision of embodied spirituality, we now argue that finding this balance is intimately connected with a process of centring and trans-centring. It is through these concepts that we aim to give the wrestling of the patients a deeper and more meaningful perspective.

To do justice to and to show our appreciation of the many stories and experiences that patients shared with us, we now review and pull together some of the basic elements that characterise their struggle as they sought to find a balance to cope with their illness. Listening to their stories, we recognised that there were a number of themes which are essential in this process.

- *Struggling with Reality-as-it-is:* This reality is very different from all earlier thoughts, hopes and expectations about it. We view this struggle as the basic aspect of embodied spirituality as a process.
- *Becoming aware of the finiteness of life:* This awareness is triggered by the life-threatening nature of the disease, making 'finiteness' an unavoidable element of Reality itself.
- *Fundamentally changing the view of Reality and the experience of Self:* Awareness of the finiteness of life uproots old, familiar and trusted frameworks of meaning and all that has up to now formed a person's identity. They no longer offer any support and make it therefore necessary for the patient to undergo a fundamental reorientation.

- *Grieving:* Letting go of trusted and familiar frameworks of meaning and identity involves a grieving process and is often accompanied by intense emotions. Grieving is an intense emotional and profoundly physical process.
- *Oscillating between opposite poles:* In the initial phase of searching for a new relationship to Reality-as-it-is and to one's own self, contradictory emotions and thoughts constantly swing back and forth, changing very rapidly.

The vision of a lived and embodied spirituality that we present in this chapter means having to say farewell to an illusory relationship to reality and an unrealistic sense of self. The challenge lies in achieving a more balanced attitude towards life and death and a more realistic sense of self. One-sided, antagonistic thoughts, feelings and activities have to be acknowledged and abandoned. Previously tenaciously held positions are exposed as extreme and illusory. They need to be transcended. It appeared from our interviews that a certain mental receptivity is needed to attain a 'middle ground'.

It became clear that finding a balance between extreme positions involves a centripetal, a centring process towards and around a 'centre'.

The universal importance of the patients' experiences

The vision of spirituality which has been unfolding in this book should not be regarded as something that is exclusively for patients with cancer or for people suffering from a life-threatening disease. All spirituality is essentially a physically embedded spirituality because human beings cannot separate themselves from their bodies.

The existentialist philosophers repeatedly hammered home the fact of 'being-a body' as a basic truth of human existence. When exploring the relationship between body and mind among patients with cancer, we need to realise that all of them are very much confronted with the painful truth of 'being-a-body' and know first-hand what it means to be a vulnerable, mortal human being.

Although some of us may not know directly what it means to be confronted with a life-threatening illness, the truth is that we do share the same basic 'condition humaine'. Everyone's life is finite and all of us have to give the reality of death a place in our minds. We have to look our mortality in the face. This is exactly what existential phenomenology stresses, especially in the writings of Heidegger. We will now turn to the contribution of his thinking in the development of our vision of embodied spirituality.

Centring as a psycho-physical movement in becoming a subject

Contribution from existential phenomenology

In our excursion into existential phenomenology, Heidegger teaches us that in consciously confronting and facing our mortality we are also offered a unique opportunity to step out of the bland and mediocre life, where we are just 'one of them', in order to become a real 'I-self', i.e. a true subject. From our reading of Heidegger, we understand that it is only when we confront our physical mortality that we grasp the reality that we are 'incarnated' in a body. Then we discover that our body is not only useful as an instrument and something to be sensuously enjoyed, but is also vulnerable and mortal.

In forming our vision of a lived and embodied spirituality, we interpreted Heidegger's 'becoming a subject', not only as a moment of incarnation in the body but also as a psychological 'centring', a unifying of necessary psychic powers for confronting death. Centring also means finding a 'middle ground' in order to bear extreme existential contradictions and go beyond them.

For example, on the one hand, going beyond the naïve idea that we have 'all the time in the world' and on the other hand the dramatic idea that we are going to die tomorrow. Both positions are illusory. Finding a more realistic middle ground between such extreme positions brings a special content to 'centring' as a concept through which the spiritual process of the patients can be identified and explored.

We visualise this centring dynamic in figure 1 below. In this figure, we have attempted to summarise the essence of the philosophy of existential phenomenology, of becoming a subject through the confrontation with the finiteness of life. At the same time, it visualises the way in which cancer patients struggle with finiteness and their death as a centripetal movement that leads them away from extreme and antagonistic positions, towards a centre where these extremes find a balance and patients become anchored in themselves.

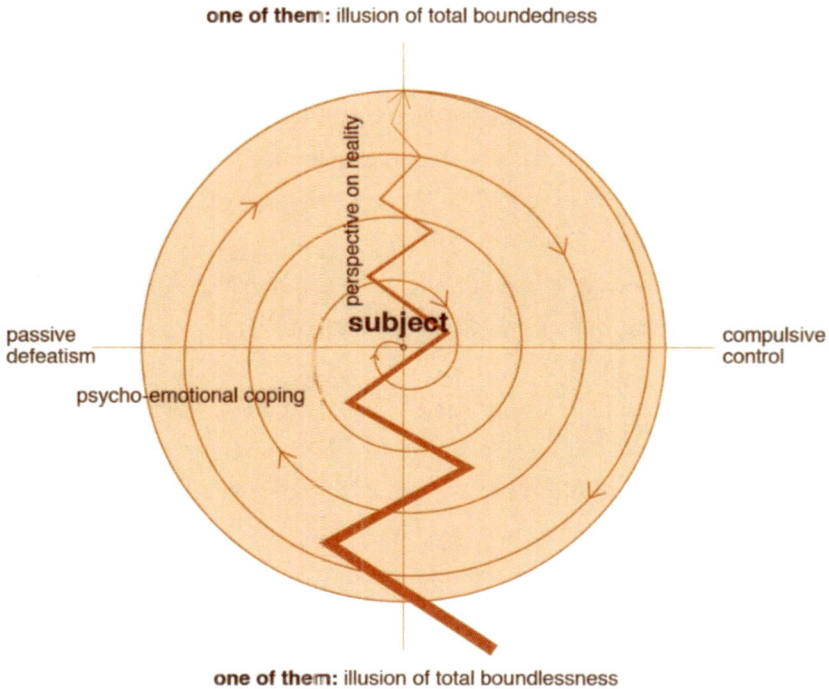

one of them: illusion of total boundedness

perspective on reality

passive
defeatism

compulsive
control

subject

psycho-emotional coping

one of them: illusion of total boundlessness

Figure 1

Centring oneself: becoming a 'subject' in the face of death

Explanation of the figure

- *The vertical axis represents the view of Reality:* The bottom position on the vertical axis is the perspective in which *one (as one of them)* lives with the illusion of boundlessness and the idea of having 'all the time in the world'. The top position is the perspective in which *one* lives in the illusion of acute finiteness and total boundedness.
- *The horizontal axis represents the experience of the Self:* The right-hand position represents the (hyper) active attitude and the compulsion to control and manipulate everything and everybody. The left-hand position is the place of defeatist powerlessness, when *one* resigns oneself to the hopelessness of the situation.

- *The zigzagging arrow moves from the illusion of boundlessness to the idea of acute finiteness:* The arrow, drawn like a bolt of lightning, symbolises the sudden realisation of one's finiteness at the diagnosis of having a life-threatening illness.
- *The centripetal line moves from being 'one of them' to being a subject:* This line visualises the dialectical, centring process, the movement from the extreme, polarised positions just described, to a position in the middle, i.e. the centre.
- *The centre:* In the midst of the contradictions, the individual comes to a place of being more centred, becoming a subject.

The above figure shows how patients are initially swept 'back and forth' between extremely contradictory positions, of thinking that they have all the time in the world or being dead tomorrow; and of thinking that they have everything under control or feeling powerless and completely defeated.

It also shows how this dramatically oscillating movement transforms itself into a process where opposite poles gradually move towards each other, towards a 'middle ground', a centre. This centripetal movement occurs simultaneously in the perspective of Reality and in the experience of the Self. It is, in fact, an interaction between these two dimensions where the one influences the other.

We, of course, describe here an ideal-typical process. Sadly, not all patients find their way from one of the extremes towards a centre, but get stuck in one of the extremes.

Becoming a subject: an essential aspect of embodied spirituality

In conclusion, we can say that lived spirituality is, according to Merleau-Ponty, incarnated in the body and according to Heidegger, incarnated in a mortal body. We see this as a centring process, where major contradictions need to be recognised, experienced and reconciled in a middle position. In facing mortality, human beings have to 'centre' themselves within themselves, becoming in this way true subjects.

By integrating Heidegger's idea of becoming a subject, our initial view of embodied spirituality gained more depth and greater existential impact than we saw at the beginning of the research journey.

The chance and the importance of becoming a subject is the crucial contribution of the existential phenomenology. It counterbalances the popularised idea that all spirituality is about getting rid of the ego.

Centring as an energetic movement of becoming a 'cosmic human being'

Contribution from Qi Gong

"Suddenly, I heard the beating of my heart and I thought, this is a part of nature here within me. And then I felt that I myself was part of nature ..."

In Chapter Six, we introduced Qi Gong as a practice that is exemplary of Chinese Daoist thinking. Qi Gong leaves space for experiences of transcendence, for which existential phenomenology allows little or no place. In that regard, it could be argued that existential phenomenology exemplifies the mind-set of the modern age that has yielded to a view of life where only what is visible, measurable and countable is considered real.

In the perspective of Qi Gong, the experience of being part of a larger whole, whether visible or invisible, is accepted as a natural and basic fact of life. Every human being stands 'in the middle' between heaven and earth. This experience of being 'in the middle' is reflected in the way a Qi Gong practitioner experiences the body, which is deeply connected with heaven and earth and also with the world around, nature and cosmos.

The experience of being 'in the middle' is also reflected in sensing the body in and from the middle of it, its centre, the *dantian*. In the practice of Qi Gong, all exercises start and return to this centre. This physical centring in Qi Gong has therefore a different content than the psychological centring in existential philosophy, where centring means becoming a subject in a finite and essentially materialistic world.

The Qi Gong practitioner experiences, in and from the centre of the body, a transcending movement that opens up to the world around, to nature and even a cosmic reality. *Dantian* is a gateway, a passage through physical reality towards a greater and encompassing Reality.

In Daoist philosophy, that underlies Qi Gong, the human being mirrors as a Microcosmos the Macrocosmos. Every fibre and organ in the body is intrinsically connected with the dimension of the cosmos. Developing a sense of self as part of this greater whole, the Qi Gong practitioner becomes a 'cosmic being' or, in Chinese, a *zhen ren*, a true human being. This presupposes developing a state of *Wu Wei*, an inner balance between action and non-action.

A number of patients have very similar experiences, whilst they do not refer to themselves as a 'cosmic being' and certainly not as a *zhen ren*. They mention feeling part of a greater whole and thereby experience energies that flow from the outside—nature, earth, cosmos, God—in and through their body.

This experience of energy is particularly prevalent among patients who participated in psycho-energetic bodywork. These patients also have the experience of feeling more centred in the middle of their body (through the psycho-energetic exercises). They also indicate that, through being in touch with this centre, they find themselves more open to the space around them.

The experience of these patients transcends the inner-worldly, horizontal-immanent dimension of the existential-phenomenological perspective. They also report that being anchored in the centre of their body helps them to stay closer to themselves in stressful circumstances, such as during certain medical treatments or visits to the doctor's office.

We visualised the centring dynamic of Qi Gong in figure 2. In it, the essence of the Daoist world view and view of the human being is made visible. Centring in Qi Gong practice implies a movement towards a psycho-spiritual centre, which is at the same time opens up to the world around.

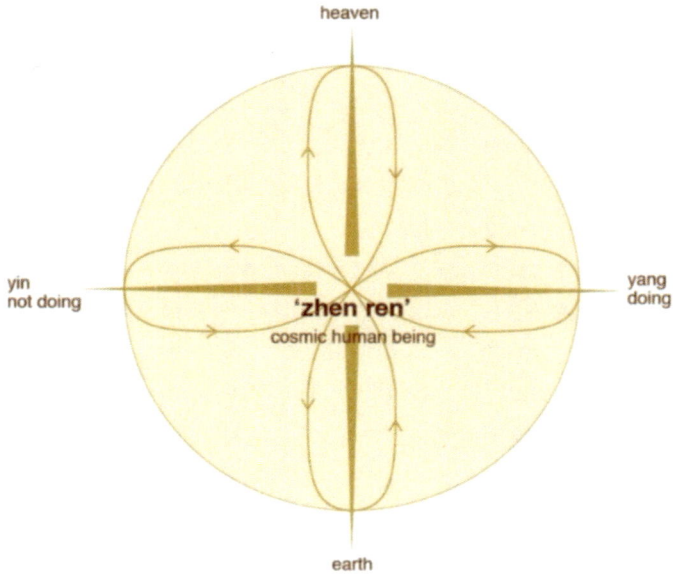

Figure 2

Centring in the middle of the body: becoming 'zhen ren', a cosmic human being

Explanation of the figure:

- *The vertical axis represents the view of reality:* The bottom position on the vertical axis is the perspective in which we know ourselves as connected to the Earth and part of earthly reality. The upper position on this axis is the perspective in which we know ourselves connected to Heaven and part of a 'heavenly', i.e. a transcendent and energetic reality.

- *The horizontal axis represents the experience of the Self in dealing with the Reality of Heaven and Earth;* The right-hand side of the horizontal axis represents 'doing' or the 'yang': the active attitude towards Reality. The left-hand side on this axis represents the 'not doing' or the 'yin': the passive-receptive attitude towards Reality.

- *The centre:* This is where the human being stands between Heaven and Earth. It is also the active merging of 'doing' and the passive of 'not doing', which is the principle of *Wu Wei*. In particular, it means being centred in the middle of the body.

The movement that is described and visualised in the above figure is very different from that in previous figure 1, where the struggle to face finiteness and death was visualised in being swept back and forth between existential extremes. Qi Gong involves an on-going, dedicated and patient process in order to go within and disconnect with the distractions of the outside world. It involves a movement down from the head, where a multitude of worries and thoughts are fostered and at the same time, from the heart where the turmoil of emotional disturbances and passions churn around.

In Chapter Six, we described Qi Gong practice as a continuous effort to strengthen the wisdom (*Yi*) mind and weaken the emotional (*Xin*) mind. This is made possible by becoming centred in the *Dantian*, in the lower region of the belly. It is in and through that centre that a connection opens up towards the surrounding space of nature and cosmos.

In conclusion, we can say that Qi Gong also complements and deepens our vision of embodied spirituality. It allows space for the experiences of transcendence of which our patients speak. The perspective of Qi Gong is not limited to the reality of being incarnated in the mortal body, nor to the subject (the I-self) as it is defined in existential phenomenology.

Qi Gong implies a movement of transcendence that goes beyond simply being the subject whose scope does not reach further than an inner-worldly, horizontal-immanent horizon. Being part of a larger whole, about which our patients speak, is a natural and healthy experience that should be taken seriously as a sign of being a real and healthy human being.

Widening the space that in existential phenomenology was accorded to the subject can now be welcomed as a next step in the development of our vision of a lived and embodied spirituality.

Trans-centring as becoming a 'person' existing in two dimensions.

The contribution of hesychasm

"Yes, I am part of the whole, but I don't dissolve. I'm not anywhere anymore. I am here, I am part of the whole and now, I am going to play the piano ... then, at another moment, I am the mother of a daughter."

Qi Gong and existential phenomenology give the impression of being two totally antagonistic ways of looking at the world and viewing the human being in it. This antagonism is reflective of modern times where the 'scientific' worldview is considered to be realistic, having a 'down-to-earth', immanent perspective on the world, whilst the 'spiritual' perspective is viewed as 'other-worldly' and transcendent.

The reason why we included hesychasm in the development of our vision on embodied spirituality is because we saw in it a paradigm in which these antagonistic perspectives could be integrated. In spite of hesychasm being clothed in the religious language of the first centuries of Christianity, the Fathers of the early Church also struggled to come to grips with the same contradictions regarding matter and mind, material and immaterial reality.

In the language of hesychasm, these were the contradictory realities of earth and heaven, humankind and God. The battle that was fought in those centuries is not that different from the battle fought in our modern era between science and religion, reason and feeling, hard facts and subjective experience. In the early Church, this struggle revolved around Jesus Christ. The key question in those days was: Was he a human being or god?

It seems that human thinking, whether today or centuries ago, can only function in 'either—or' schemes. To think of two opposites being true at the same time goes beyond our thinking capacity. It is like those famous koans in Japanese Zen Buddhism in which the reasoning mind is deliberately derailed and challenged to go beyond itself. To get a glimpse of Reality-as-it-is, it is necessary to let go of the thinking mind. It has to be given up.

Also, the early Fathers of the Church and their theologians challenged themselves to go beyond their reasoning minds and accept the paradox of Jesus Christ as being human and divine at the same time: two 'natures', yet one person. Two contradictory realities being united and true at the same time. The theologians of that era affirmed that this was not only true of Jesus Christ but also of every human being. Therefore, according to these Church Fathers, in the depth of our being we are all a living paradox, mortal and immortal, defined by finiteness yet infinite and divine.

The paradigm of hesychast thinking provides a way of reconciling the antagonism of the finite and mortal subject within existential phenomenology and the cosmic human being, whose inner essence, according to Qi Gong stretches into infinity. The term *trans-centring* is introduced here to make a connection possible between the two truths of being a subject and a cosmic being.

In existential phenomenology, we saw that a human being, when he has the courage to face his mortality, centres himself psychologically in his being a subject. In Qi Gong, centring is also a very important movement, where it has a very physical content as centring in the midst of the body. But it does not stop there. The centring movement goes right through the psycho-physical centre, making the body's centre a gateway to a greater whole, a transcendent reality.

In Qi Gong practice, this sense of being part of a greater whole is a real experiential reality. This was also true for several patients who committed themselves to the exercises offered in psycho-energetic bodywork. Fully aware of their mortality—and being a subject in the way Heidegger described it—they felt supported and embraced by a greater whole. They had somehow learned to go towards and right through the centre of their body and themselves, opening to a greater whole. In other words, they had learned to 'trans-centre'.

This trans-centring process is beautifully visualised in the icon of the Transfiguration that shows the intimate connection, even interpenetration, of two contradictory realities. A clear difference between Qi Gong and hesychasm is that in the former the cosmic energies are an impersonal force, whilst in the latter they are seen as the energies flowing out of the Godhead (*energeiai theou*), actively seeking entrance into the soul and heart of the human being. It is the *inter-action* of these two realities that distinguishes hesychasm from Qi Gong. Before returning to the icon, we will first visualise the centripetal dynamism of hesychasm in figure 3.

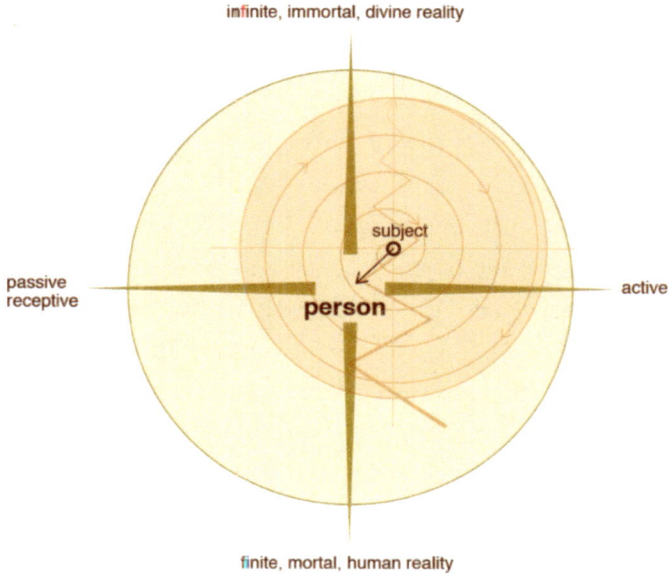

Figure 3

Trans-centring: becoming-a-person through integrating contradictions

Explanation of the figure:

- *The vertical axis represents Reality, which, at the same time, is finite and infinite:* The bottom position on the vertical axis represents the view on Reality as finite, mortal, human. The top position on this axis represents the view on Reality as infinite, immortal, divine. Each pole in itself represents only a limited aspect of total Reality.

- *The horizontal axis represents the experience of the Self in dealing with this Reality:* The right-hand position on the horizontal axis represents the active relation to Reality. The left-hand position on this axis represents the passive-receptive relationship thereto.

- *The intersecting axes in the large circle:* The vertical axis represents the potential connection between the opposites in the view of Reality. The horizontal axis represents the potential connection between the opposites in the experience of the Self.

- *The centre of the large circle:* This reflects the coming together of the infinite and finite, divine and human Reality. It is also the coming together of the active and passive/receptive relationship of the Self to this reality. The middle represents the reconciliation and integration of the opposites.

- *The arrow from the subject to the centre of the large circle:* In this picture, the *subject* is recognisable in the small, darker circle. The *person* is represented by the bigger, wider circle. The passage through the centre of the *subject* to the other dimension of *being a person* is made visible with an obliquely downward-pointing arrow. This arrow goes through the centre of the smaller circle to the centre of the larger one. The *subject* is not undone, but becomes transparent to a comprehensive Reality.

This trans-centring dynamic of hesychasm forms the final step in the development of our vision of embodied spirituality. The trans-centring process that goes through the middle of the body is, at the same time, a movement through the horizontal-immanent reality of the *subject* into the vertical-transcendent reality of *the cosmic human being*. And vice-versa!

The *subject* of existential phenomenology can be seen from the perspective of hesychasm as the human being in human nature.

The *cosmic human being* of Qi Gong can be seen from the perspective of hesychasm as man in his divine nature.

It is the mutual inter-penetration of these dimensions that forms the very essence of being a person.

Conclusion: *Embodied spirituality as a process of profound transformation*

Becoming-a-person: the trans-centring dynamic of embodied spirituality

It can be said that embodied spirituality, when dealing with a life-threatening illness, involves finding a balance between the illusionary idea of having all the time in the world and the fear of imminent death. Patients also swing between the urge to keep everything under control and the sense of being completely powerless and helpless.

Embodied spirituality is the arduous process of accepting Reality-as-it-is. It implies a centripetal, i.e. a centre directed process in finding a middle position between and beyond seemingly contradictory positions like fight and surrender, fear and trust. In this process, the reality of mortality must be given a place, as must the realisation that life is not under control. Unrealistic ideas and fantasies about life and the self must be abandoned. Our dialogue with the three external philosophical/spiritual traditions underscores this and sees embodied spirituality as a process of profound transformation:

Existential phenomenology emphasises the need for the awareness of bounded finitude. Therefore, the step must be taken to truly accept the vulnerable, mortal body, which means becoming truly incarnated. The courage to face one's own death involves the transition from life lived as *one of them* to a life truly lived as *a subject,* with a realistic view of the Self and Reality-as-it-is. This subject is Heidegger's *Ich-selbst*, I-self. Despite the common exhortation to get rid of the 'ego', embodied spirituality actually means becoming what we are destined to be: an incarnated, courageous I-self.

Qi Gong honours the un-bounded experience of becoming a *cosmic man*, a being who knows himself as part of a larger whole. This is not an abstract philosophical idea, but an actual—even physical and energetic—lived experience. In this perspective, incarnation implies a deeper experience of the body. Not only is physical boundedness realised but also the space beyond the bounded, delineated form of this body. Characteristic of Qi Gong practice is that the experience of being centred in the middle of the body unlocks the passage into an unlimited, all-encompassing transcendent space: nature, earth, heaven and cosmos.

Hesychasm provides a paradigm that offers space to accommodate these apparent contradictory experiences: that of being a *subject* and a *cosmic human being*, bounded and unbounded, finite and infinite. In the Christology that underlies the entire practice of hesychasm, it is precisely the coming together of these two realities that makes a (wo)man a *person*.

In this personhood, the *subject* of existential phenomenology is not undone, but honoured, whilst at the same time space is given to the *cosmic human being* of Qi Gong. In the terminology of hesychasm, this points to the coming together of the human and divine nature of man and God.

We conclude from this that the struggle to accept Reality-as-it-is involves a profound transformation of becoming the courageous *subject* of existential phenomenology, the *cosmic human being (zhen ren)* of Qi Gong and the human-divine *person* of hesychasm.

This study into the relationship between the body and spirituality not only provides insight into the lived spirituality of a certain group of patients. It is also significant for a more universal understanding of spirituality, because all spirituality is, in fact, embodied. It is made repeatedly clear that spirituality is not limited to a striving for higher, infinite and exceptional dimensions of life, but is, for every person, a struggle with Reality-as-it-is.

Embodied spirituality: a process of profound transformation

- Embodied spirituality involves an ongoing transformation in which ever-deeper dimensions of incarnation are unlocked and in which the dichotomy between mind and body is radically undone. *The vulnerable and mortal body* is man's honest confrontation with life's finiteness. *The sensory-energetic body* is open to a transcendent dimension beyond the confines of the body and life itself. *The trans-centred, transfigured body* encompasses the immanent and transcendent dimensions of life, its finiteness and its inherent infinity.
- Embodied spirituality involves a transformation, leading away from illusory ideas about life, towards Reality-as-it-is. This can mean that human existence can sometimes be frightening and appalling and yet at other times grand and wondrous.
- Embodied spirituality involves a transformation in the experience of the Self. It leads away from false and unrealistic ideas that need to be shed in order to find the true self, the person who dares to live, in the midst of paradox.

Being a person does not mean having attained a well-defined identity, something that is actually always out of reach. The inherent limitless, transcendent aspect of Reality never allows a person's identity to be definitively defined.[71] An embodied spirituality is a never-ending journey of letting go of who we think we are. But the journey is never meaningless or futile.

---

[71] This refusal to give a final description of who and what we are in the depths of our being is in fact an 'anthropologia negativa' just as there is a 'theologia negativa' that refuses to formulate the deepest essence of God.

As we constantly have to let go of ideas and notions of ourselves, we become more and more the mystery that we are in our deepest being. Embodied spirituality involves an endless process of ***Losing me, becoming 'me'.*** Hence the title of this book.

Our Vision Visualised in the Icon
of the Transfiguration

Blueprint for the human person

None of the authors in Eastern or Western theology, writing about the icon of the Transfiguration, attribute any special significance to the centre in the pelvic area of the Christ figure. From the perspective of Daoist Qi Gong, this is a crucial place, namely the lower Dantian, the true physical and psycho-energetic centre in man.[72] It is the area where cosmic energies are absorbed, concentrated and from which they radiate into the space around the body.

In a similar way, it is characteristic of the iconography of hesychasm that in the middle of Christ's body, a centre of energy is depicted as a blinding light, radiating from there in all directions around him. Right through the centre of his physical body, a passageway is opened into a space of infinity, God. It is a two-way movement, in which everything that is human and everything that is divine interact and intertwine. In the classic formula of the Council of Chalcedon: the coming together of two 'natures' in one 'person'.

Qi Gong practice offers a host of exercises to get in touch with this centre in the middle of the body. The psycho-energetic exercises the patients talked about have the same purpose and go even a step farther than Qi Gong practice. Both practices support a form of spirituality that is truly and deeply embodied. In this spirituality, the cultivation of a lived contact with the body and the body's centre is crucial. When this centre in the depth of one's body is found and brought into consciousness, the dichotomy between body and mind—and even between the human being and God—is undone.

---

[72] It is interesting that on the icon the centre of the cross is even lower than the lower than *Dantian*. This centre coincides with the focus of psycho-energetic body work.

146

For the purpose of better understanding and valuing the paradigm underlying hesychasm, the previously posted figure 3 is projected over the body of Christ as depicted on the icon of the Transfiguration. This is figure 4 printed below.

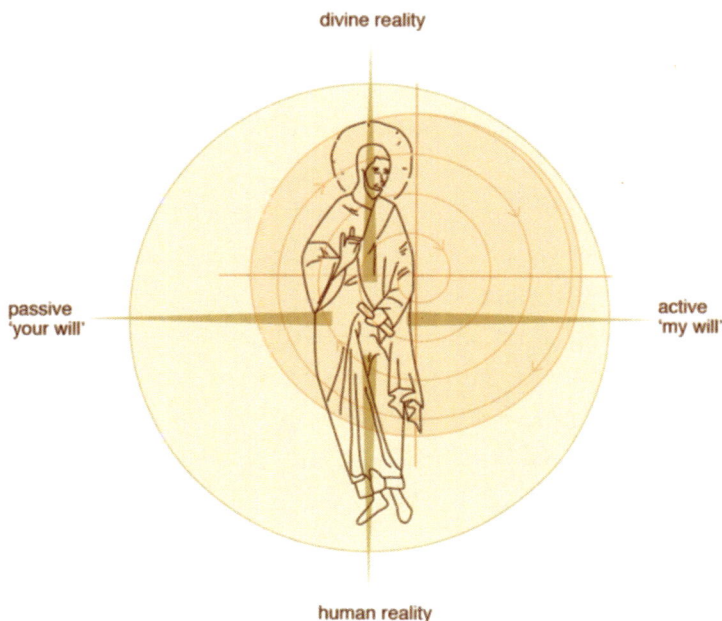

Figure 4
Trans-centring and the icon of the Transfiguration.

The dynamic pattern of the centring and even trans-centring process of coping with a life-threatening illness (see: Figure 3) is combined with the static pattern of the icon. Both patterns offer their own perspective and complement each other.

The first pattern shows the dynamics of the spiritual process as a path away from living in an illusory reality towards living Reality-as-it-is. It is a centripetal movement, away from the contradictions at the periphery of life to a centre. It is often a painful and often very oscillating process of being thrown back and forth and up and down, between resistance and surrender.

In this last image, in which the centring and trans-centring process is projected over the figure of the Tabor icon, this icon is now presented as a blueprint for the human being on the way of becoming a *person*. In the tradition of hesychasm, this means that the human being is invited to mirror this icon. A meditation on this icon can bring about, as it were, an energetic 'imitatio Christi' at a physical-energetic, psychological and spiritual level.

The icon makes visible that every human being lives within a concrete horizontal-immanent reality without being limited by it. At the same time, the human being is also part of a transcendent reality without dissolving into it, therefore living simultaneously in a horizontal-immanent and vertical-transcendent reality.

What is made visible in the image we present here is that access to this unity-in-duality involves a trans-centring dynamic. This dynamic permeates, deepens and enriches the being the subject of existential phenomenology and the simply being part of a larger whole of Qi Gong. This is the ultimate transformation involved in a lived and embodied spirituality.

In this way, the icon can be freed of its holiness and seen as a blueprint for the human *person* or for the process of *becoming a person*. This could also make the icon interesting and even relevant to those who do not have (or no longer have) any connection with the Christian faith.

Relevance of this Research to the Fields of Cancer Care and Christian Spirituality

The field of cancer(oncological) care

The relevance of this book to the field of cancer care (oncology) can be distinguished according to medical treatment, psycho-social support and pastoral care:

- *Medical treatment* should not become fixated purely on the affected part of the body. The patient is a *person* and should be regarded as such. Patients often describe being treated and viewed like objects within a fixed and standardised medical protocol. This has a depersonalising effect and gets in the way of having to deal with the existential challenge that having a life-threatening illness involves.
- P*sycho-social support* should not pathologize the patient's fear of death and the emotional distress this can bring and not immediately label them according to the DSM V psychiatric categories. Patients' feelings and experiences should be seen primarily as part of the intense oscillating nature of the existential search triggered by having a life-threatening illness. Caregivers need to be able to honour and value how it is for those living with cancer. They need to allow space for the fear and distress of their patients, endure these and dare to remain 'present', being in a close and compassionate contact with their patients' existential struggle.
- *Pastoral care* should not simply be limited to ministering the word, administering sacraments or offering a listening ear. Pastoral care could also involve offering some form of psycho-energetic body work to patients (see Appendix). It is through the body that patients can access a transcendent dimension in which the fear of death can be reduced.

The relevance of this study for Christian spirituality consists in recognising the crucial importance of the body and the experience of the body within the process of a truly embodied spirituality. Embodied spirituality is not about achieving an 'exalted' spiritual state of mind, but involves a profound struggle with Reality, which is always different to what is expected or imagined.

Letting go of the familiar view of reality (even one's faith in a good God), learning to accept how life IS, rather than how it ought to be, trusting that it is possible to live in the midst of life's contradictions and polarities, are all part and parcel of a lived and embodied spirituality.

Embodied spirituality is ultimately about 'becoming' who you really are; it is a work in progress. In becoming a true *person*, living in a finite immanent and infinite transcendent Reality, the uniqueness of personhood is not erased but comes into its own right when these seemingly contradictory two dimensions of Reality are embraced.

To conclude

This study shows that a dialogue with philosophical and spiritual traditions in which the body occupies a crucial place is meaningful and even necessary. It opens a perspective on to a physical-energetic aspect of spirituality from which the Christian tradition in the West has, over the centuries, virtually shied away from.

In particular, the dialogue with the Orthodox East can bring to the fore the physical-mystical nature of Christianity and the icon of the Transfiguration offers a blueprint for this. It points to an inner space, to the most inner space of the human body. It is from out of that space that a passage opens up to a greater Reality, to God. This involves a deeply transformative process of 'trans-centring', of going right through the centre of the body and of the self as a subject. By projecting the icon into the space of one's own body, a new and more embodied form of an 'imitatio Christi' emerges.

The research detailed in this book is a response to the plea of the German theologian Walter Kasper to bridge the separation between faith and life that originated in modern times. According to Kasper, this separation reflects the dichotomy that permeates the entirety of modern culture, namely that between spirit and matter, subject and object, god and world.

As a result, the external world in its totality has been reduced to inanimate matter which, under the influence of science and technology, is subject to the arbitrariness of human intervention. The question of whether theology and the Christian church still have any relevance for our time will depend, according to Kasper, on the contribution they can make to the healing of this separation. Of decisive significance is the renewed rethinking of the theme of the Council of Chalcedon and the impact of the Incarnation of God in the human being of Jesus Christ.

This study, with its focus on the relationship of the experience of the body and a lived and embodied spirituality, seeks to contribute to the healing of this separation.

Appendix
Psycho-Energetic Bodywork

The text of this book regularly refers to psycho-energetic therapy as the form of bodywork that was offered in Tabor House, Nijmegen, as part of psycho-social counselling.[73] In addition to counselling sessions and haptonomic massages, psycho-energetic therapy formed an integrated part of the programme. The experiences of transcendence described in Chapter Four appeared to occur frequently amongst patients who participated in this therapy. The following is a brief description of psycho-energetic bodywork.

History of the psycho-energetic bodywork

Psycho-energetic bodywork is rooted in a western, particularly European tradition. The practice began in the nineteenth century as a reaction against a culture that had become more and more hostile towards the body, increasingly suffocating all human spontaneity and leading to the body literally and figuratively being tightly corseted. The impetus for this counter-cultural response was initiated by the French singing teacher, Francois Delsarte (1811–1871).

This impulse from France was taken up by a number of German breathing therapists and remedial gymnasts, such as Hede Kallmeyer, Elsa Gindler, Alice Schaarschuch and especially Ilse Middendorf. They were also perhaps reacting against the wide-spread Prussian-militaristic methods of education in their home

---

[73] Staps, T. and Yang, W. (1991) *Psycho-energetische Therapie: psychosociale begeleiding van kankerpatiënten,* Nijkerk: INTRO.
Yang, W. (2021) *Yoga of Courage and Compassion, Conscious Breathing and Guided Meditation,* Rochester, Vermont: Inner Traditions.

country. In America, Genevieve Stebbins spread Delsarte's ideas, which were taken up by and integrated into the training of actors.

This different way of relating to the body was also introduced into the world of dance and adopted by the renowned dancer Isadora Duncan (1878–1927) and the Czech-German dance pedagogue Rudolf von Laban de Varalya (1879–1959).[74]

The work of Gerda Alexander, Alice Schaarschuch[75] and Ilse Middendorf[76] further refined and explored this body culture. Robert van Heeckeren[76] introduced the work of Schaarschuch and Middendorf into the Netherlands in the 1960s, integrating this into a form of yoga that was more adapted to European culture than the traditional forms of yoga coming from the Indian continent.

For a psychological and philosophical justification of this European bodywork, Ilse Middendorf in particular referred to the ideas of C.G. Jung and the 'Existentiallehre' of Karlfried Graf von Dürckheim.[77]

The psycho-energetic bodywork described in this book is mainly based on the work of Hetty Draayer, who was a student of Dürckheim and later developed her unique form of bodywork and breathing meditation. When she herself was confronted with cancer and had to deal with her own existential crisis, she developed in-depth insight into the energetic anatomy of the human being, whose energy pathways and centres she could suddenly 'see'.

An important aspect of her work was the focus she placed on opening a centre, deep in the space of the pelvis. She describes this in the following way: "In the centre of our body, deep within the space of the pelvis, lies the 'cosmic

---

[74] This is a brief summary of historical surveys as described in the books of H. Kallmeyer, *Heil Kraft durch Bewegung und Atem,* (Heidelberg, Karl F. Haug Verlag, 1970) and from I. Middendorf, *Der Erfahrbare Atem: eine Atemlehre,* (Paderborn, Junfermann Verlag, 1984) and *Der erfahrbare Atem in seiner Substanz,* (Paderborn: Junfermann Verlag, 2008).

[75] A. Schaarschuch, A. (1995) *Der atmende Mensch,* Bietigheim:TurmVerlag. (Dutch translation. *De ademende mens,* Deventer: Ankh-Hermes, 1976).

[76] Robert van Heeckeren did not publish his work. He integrated into classical Hatha Yoga the natural breathing theory of Alice Schaarschuch.

[77] von Dürckheim, K. (1967) *Hara: Die Erdmitte des Menschen,* Weilheim: Otto Wilhelm Barth-Verlag. (English translation, *Hara: The vital Center of* Man, Rochester: Inner Traditions, 2004).
von Dürckheim, K. (1968) Überweltliches Leben in der Welt, Weilheim: Otto Wilhelm Barth-Verlag.

eye'. When we learn to breathe, meditate and live from this point, all the pores of the skin open, our body is transformed into energy and all of our cells vibrate in harmony with the cosmic energy flowing through us."[78]

Development of psycho-energetic bodywork

Psycho-energetic bodywork is a continuation of the specific bodywork as this developed across Europe. Over time, it was seen to be of benefit to various groups, including people with cancer and other life-threatening diseases. The needs and requirements of this special group helped to determine the content of this form of bodywork.

During the first period of its development (1983–1989), it was offered at the Canisius-Wilhelmina Hospital, Nijmegen, to patients who required chemotherapy. The aim was to help them tolerate better the negative side effects of chemotherapy. Elements from existing forms of bodywork were used, in so far as they were considered appropriate for each patient. It was never the intention to blindly apply a particular method simply because it was believed to be beneficial for everybody.

After first establishing a trusted person-to-person contact, psycho-energetic bodywork begins with simple relaxation and breathing exercises and develops from there. A further benefit of the exercises was that they gave patients the feeling of being able to influence their own physical and psychological well-being.

During the second period of its development (1990–2000) the psycho-energetic bodywork was offered at Tabor House and came to be regarded as an essential part of its psycho-social counselling programme, which also included psychotherapeutic counselling and haptonomic massage. This form of bodywork helped patients to accept, endure and tolerate intense emotions and to learn to let go of obsessive thoughts by anchoring the mind in the body, which only exists in the here and now.

---

[78] Draayer, H. (2010) *Meditatie, energie en bewustzijn: De innerlijke weg vanuit het kosmisch oog,* Rotterdam: De Driehoek.
H. Draayer, H. (2007) *Finde dich selbst durch Meditation, ein Lese-und Übungsbuch,* Darmstadt: Schirnerverlag.

In order for this form of bodywork to benefit patients over the long term, it was important for patients to also practice the exercises at home on a daily basis. To facilitate this, a number of basic exercises were recorded on a CD.

During the third period of its development (2000–2012) the psycho-energetic bodywork was more overtly linked to the dimension of spirituality. It became possible to talk with colleagues in the medical field about a patient's spirituality without encountering the level of resistance which the word 'spirituality' had tended to evoke during the earlier years.

Our previous research into the existential crisis in people with cancer has contributed to the growing awareness that attending to a patient's spirituality is an important factor in helping patients to cope with this life-threatening illness. It was during this third period of development that the 'Tabor Meditation Training' was developed for patients in the palliative phase and their partners.[79] It is in this phase that the confrontation with mortality becomes very concrete and initiates an intense psychospiritual process. The psycho-energetic bodywork aims to support this process.

Structure of the exercises

The psycho-energetic bodywork is made up of a series of exercises which sit within a structure that has an inner logic and is summarised in the terms:

1. Grounding
2. Centring
3. Transcending.

1. Grounding

"My energy used to be in my head. It was an intellectual, mental energy. I love it when I am once again able to feel the contact with the lower part of my body. I rediscover that I have legs to stand on and that I have a pelvis—Yes and I have also become aware of the sensation of being carried and supported by the earth! You are carried, no matter how sick you are and even when you die you

---

[79] The development of this meditation training was made possible by a financial subsidy awarded in 2009 by the province of Gelderland.

are still being carried. This is why death no longer frightens me." (woman, breast cancer, 54 years)

Restoring contact with the body in order to be more 'present' in it is fundamental to all the exercises offered within psycho-energetic bodywork. For people with a life-threatening illness, being present in their bodies is of great importance because the diagnosis of cancer often leads to a sensation of being 'shocked out of their body'. Being more present in one's own body can, of course, be very confronting, yet it creates a space in which various physical sensations and feelings can be recognised and accepted in a more neutral and less emotionally charged way. It is important to help patients refrain from judging their bodies in a negative way.

Simple relaxation exercises can be an important first step in learning to accept the body as it is. Such exercises initiate a process of 'incarnation', an immersion into the reality of the body. It involves a step towards accepting 'Reality-as-it-is', which turns out to be so very different to imagined hopes and wishes. Restoring contact with one's own body is an important counterweight to the many medical treatments, as a result of which patients often become alienated from their own body, experiencing themselves as objects of medical-technical treatment.

The relaxation exercises within psycho-energetic therapy are not an inner-directed, solipsistic event. They begin by focusing on the close environment, beginning with the 'ground' underneath, which can be the bed you lie on, the chair you sit on or the floor you stand on: ultimately with the earth beneath you. Hence the term 'grounding'.

Learning to focus on the physical reality of the body and the concrete reality of the earth beneath can open up a sense of being supported, carried and 'cared for' by the earth itself.

2. Centring

"In difficult times, I can remain peaceful and return to that point of rest within myself. Going back to the centre of my pelvis. Returning to that bowl in and around my pelvis, to that space of tranquillity. And from there feel my strength emerge—really radiate like a huge ball of light. I see it, it becomes warm and it starts to flow." (woman, breast cancer, 64 years old)

Psycho-energetic bodywork emphasises the need for a balance between tension and relaxation. It does not exclusively emphasise relaxation. Ultimately, it is about finding a middle ground between these two poles. It is about 'eutonia', a 'right and healthy tension' in body and mind. Within this right tension, the extremes of hypo-and hypertonia, the under-tension and the over-tension, are neutralised and transformed.

Also, the extremes of functioning too much at a mental or emotional level must be avoided and transcended. The same applies to being much too focused on the outside world or on oneself.

Finding this middle ground forms a basic principle of bodywork. It involves focusing attention towards the centre of the body. This was fundamental in the work of people like Dürckheim, Schaarschuch, Middendorf and Draayer. It was their experience that in this central space, an inner force can manifest itself that differs from a mental or emotional force or a force that is generated by the power of the will. In the chapters describing Qi Gong and hesychasm explicit attention was given to this bodily centre as a source of energy, power and light.

An important additional benefit is that by becoming more anchored in our body's centre of gravity, it is possible to shift the focus away from the sick or painful part of the body. The debilitating effect of intense emotions and feelings, such as the fear of death, can also, to a certain extent, be neutralised. This does not mean that all emotions and feelings dissolve and disappear forever. Rather, being more anchored in the body's centre means that emotions can be tolerated, supported and expressed in a clearer and cleaner way.

3. Transcending

"In that breathing, I experience space and light—The contours of my body fade. My body becomes more than my material body. As if you get access to another dimension." (Woman, breast cancer, 1968)

Living and breathing from the body's centre brings about a radical change in the experience of the body as a whole. The way a person breathes may also be substantially altered, leading to deeper, calmer and steadier breathing. It is a little known fact that the respiratory organs include not only the lungs but also the skin.

When the skin becomes more relaxed and hence more porous, it also seems to 'breathe' in and out. With the skin also breathing, the contours of the body seem to form less of a defined boundary and as an organ, the skin mediates between the space inside the body and the space around it. This allows for a stronger energetic exchange between the inner and outer world. This is probably why it is that through such breathing and relaxation exercises, patients sometimes describe feeling 'part of a larger whole': nature, life, the cosmos.

The relevance of this research for psycho-energetic bodywork

The terms grounding, centring and transcending acquire a deeper meaning as the intimate relationship between the changes in the experience of the body and the changes in the sense of self emerges. The transformation of the term *grounding* into 'incarnating' also has a far-reaching meaning. It makes the relationship with mortality more explicit so that a clear distinction is created from the many *wellness and fitness* programmes that are in abundance these days.

The term incarnating also resonates with the concept of Incarnation. In Chapter Seven, we described this as a central theme in the Christian tradition. We argued that psycho-energetic body work in an unexpected manner connects with the heart of Christian spirituality. This connection was completely unrecognised when our theory was first being developed. For many patients, connecting their childhood religion with an approach that fully recognises the body and their corporeality proved to be surprising, intriguing and inspiring.

In this study, the concept of *centring* gained a deeper dynamic in the term *trans-centring*. This involves more than just shifting the centre of gravity from the head to the centre in the pelvis. Rather, it means a transition to a transcendent dimension beyond the self as an autonomous subject and vice versa. Becoming open from within this centre towards two totally different dimensions and the integration of these two dimensions into 'becoming a person' is an aspect of psycho-energetic bodywork that had not been worked out before in this way.

The breathing cross

The basic pattern of psycho-energetic practice is visualised in the image printed below. This blueprint makes visible where the psycho-physical centre is located in the body as a focus of attention within the practice. This is located in the space in front of the sacrum. Focusing the attention on this centre and collecting the breath within its space *(centring)* offers a way of becoming more present in the body *(incarnating)* and from there opening up to a wider dimension of reality *(transcending)*.

This place corresponds exactly to the centre of the figure of the Christ on the Tabor icon. It should be noted that this centre is lower than the *Dantian* in Qi Gong practice and therefore, literally and figuratively, offers a deeper level of experience.

A simple exercise involves visualising a horizontal beam of energy from the centre of the body to the left and right when breathing in and visualising a vertical energy beam from the space above the head to below the feet when breathing out. These beams intersect at the centre of the pelvis, where warmth, energy or light can be experienced after practicing this exercise over a period of time.

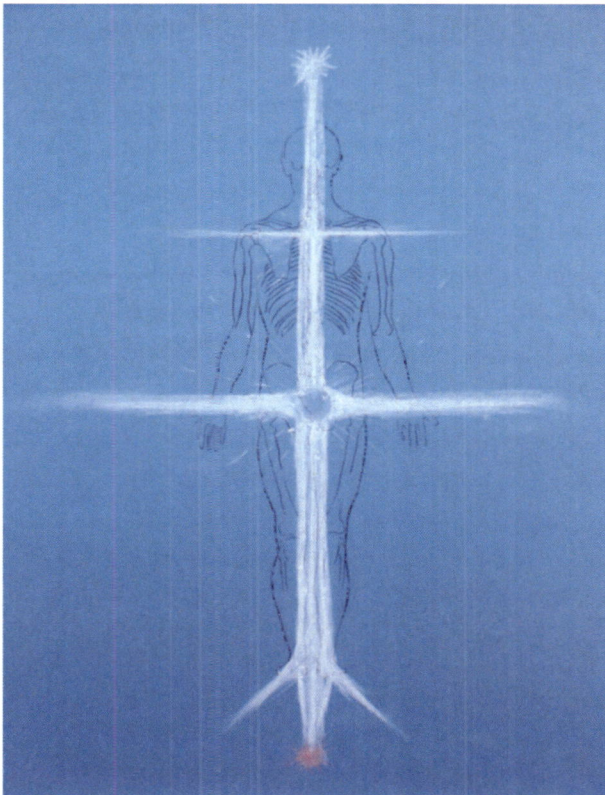

Image: Peter Kampschuur

Basic exercise from psycho-energetic bodywork

Finally, a basic exercise has been added that is taken from the work of Hetty Draayer which is a free translation of an exercise that has been included in her book *Finde dich selbst durch Meditation (Find yourself through meditation).*[80]

Lie comfortably and relaxed on a mattress or a folded blanket. When doing this, consciously roll your spine, vertebra after vertebra, down to the floor. In this way, you are able to experience more and more contact throughout the entire spine with the ground and the earth beneath you.

To relax, it can help to put a pillow under your head and a rolled-up towel under your knees. Place your feet approximately twenty inches apart and let the front part of your feet loosely fall to the sides. Place your hands on your lower abdomen just above your pubic bone. The fingers should be placed opposite to each other without touching.

Close your eyes so that you can concentrate better on breathing in and out and on feeling the flow of energies through your body. Are you aware of this energy? Can you allow and surrender yourself to them? Breathe in very quietly and try to experience more and more space in and around your pelvis. Visualise the form of a large round bowl taking shape around your pelvis. This bowl opens up a horizontal dimension within you. This horizontal dimension can only really open when you breathe out through your whole body, from the top of your head to the toes and beyond. This opens up a vertical dimension.

Let these vertical and horizontal currents of breath cross each other deep in your lower abdomen. Together, they form a pattern of a cross. The aim is to experience the area where these currents of breath cross in the depth of your pelvis more clearly. Then consider how you do not 'take' your breath, but how your in-breath 'arises' by and of itself from the depth of your pelvis and how you become spacious and wide from there. You will then see how exhaling from above your head flows through this spacious depth within the centre of your body and then out through your legs and feet.

By breathing in and out in this way, you will experience the central point of intersection of the cross in the depth of your lower abdomen and become increasingly more aware of it. At a certain point, you become so familiar with it that it will remain with you throughout the day.

More meditative exercises can be found in William Yang's (audio) book *Yoga of Courage and Compassion.* (see footnote 73)

---

[80] Draayer, H. (2007) *Finde dich selbst durch Meditation,* Darmstadt: Schirner Verlag.

Bibliography

Andreopoulos, A. (2005) *Metamorphosis: The Transfiguration in Byzantine Theology and Iconography*, New York: St. Vladimir's Seminary Press.

Armstrong, K. (1999) *A History of God.* London: Vintage Books.

Attig, Th. and Neimeyer, R. (Ed) (2001) 'Relearning the World: Making and Finding Meanings', *Meaning Reconstruction & the Experience of Loss,* Washington: American Psychological Association, 33–53.

Baart, A. (2001) *Een theorie van presentie,* Utrecht: Lemma.

Bastiaansen, L. (1984) *De Thaborikoon: Theologie and Symboliek van de Iconen,* Zundert: Abdij Maria Toevlucht.

Bolte Taylor, J. (2008) *Onverwacht inzicht: het persoonlijke verhaal van een neurologe over haar herseninfarct,* Utrecht/Antwerpen: Kosmos uitgevers.

Certeau de, M. (1966) 'Culture and spiritual experience', *Concilium* 19 no.1, 31.

Chia, M. and Chia, M. (1990) *Chi Nei Tsang, Internal Organs Chi Massage,* Huntington, MY: Healing Tao Books.

Creswell, J. W. (2003) *Research Design: Qualitative, Quantitative and Mixed Approaches,* Thousand Oaks, CA: Sage.

Denzin, N. K. (1978) *The research act,* 2nd Edition. Chicago: Aldine.

Draayer, H. (2007) *Finde dich selbst durch Meditation: ein Lese-und Übungsbuch,* Darmstadt: Schirnerverlag.

Draayer, H. (2010) *Meditatie, energie en bewustzijn: De innerlijke weg vanuit het kosmisch oog,* Rotterdam: De Driehoek.

Dürckheim von, K. (1974) *Hara: Het dragende midden van de mens,* Tweede druk, Deventer: Ankh-Hermes.

Dürckheim von, K. (1980) *Transcendentaal ervaren: De zin van volledige menswording,* Katwijk aan Zee: Servire.

Eliade, M. (1953) *Le Yoga—immortalité et liberté,* Paris: Petite Bibliothèque Payot.

Evdokimov, P. (1970) *L'art de l'Icône: théologie de la beauté,* Bruges: Desclée De Brouwer.

Evdokimov, P. (1959) *L'Orthodoxie,* Neuchatel: Bibliothèque théologique, Delachaux et Nestlé S.A.

Falsetti, S. A., Resick, P. A and Davis, J. L. (2003) 'Changes in religious beliefs following trauma', *Journal of Traumatic Stress,* 16, 4, 391–398.

Froese, K. (2006) *Nietzsche, Heidegger and Daoist Thought,* Albany: State University of New York Press.

Gadamer, H. G. (2014) *Waarheid en methode: Hoofdlijnen van een filosofische hermeneutiek,* Nijmegen: Vantilt. (Original: *Wahrheit und Methode.* Tübingen: Verlag Mohr, 1960.)

Glas, G., Goes, G., Spreeuwenberg, C., Bakker, D. and Dilman, R. (Eds) (2002) 'Existentiële vragen, angst en geloofsproblemen', *Handboek Palliatieve Zorg,* Maarssen: Elsevier Gezondheidszorg, 237–254.

Glaser, B. and Strauss, A. (1967) *Discovery of Grounded Theory,* Chicago: Aldine.

Haes de, J. (1988) *Kwaliteit van leven van kankerpatiënten,* Amsterdam: Swets and Zeitlinger.

Hagman, G. and Neimeyer, R. (Ed) (2001) 'Beyond Decathexis: Toward a New Psychological Understanding and Treatment of Mourning', *Meaning Reconstruction & the Experience of Loss,* Washington: American Psychological Association, 13–31.

Heelas, P. (2012) *Spirituality in the modern World, Within Religious Tradition and Beyond,* Abingdon—New York: Routledge.

Heidegger, M. (1963) *Sein und Zeit,* 10th edition, Tübingen: Max Niemeyer Verlag.

Hennezel de, M. (1996) *De intieme dood: Levenslessen van stervenden,* 2nd Edition, Haarlem: J.H. Gottmer/H.J.W, Becht BV.

Hense, E. and Maas, F. (Eds) (2011) 'Introduction', *Towards a Theory of Spirituality. Studies in Spirituality*, Supp 22, Titus Brandsma Institute, Leuven: Peeters, 1–4.

Hense, E. and Maas, F. (Eds) (2011) 'The quest for interdisciplinary theories on spirituality', *Towards a Theory of Spirituality. Studies in Spirituality*, Supp 22, Titus Brandsma Institute, Leuven: Peeters.

Hense, E., Jespers, F. and Nissen, P. (Eds) (2014) 'Present-day Spiritualities in Confessional, Popular, Professional and Aesthetic Contexts: Contrasts or Overlap?' *Present-Day Spiritualities, contrasts and overlaps,* Boston: Brill, 1–17.

Heyde, L. (1995) *Het gewicht van de eindigheid: Over de filosofische vraag naar God,* Amsterdam: Boom.

Heyde, L. (2000) *De Maat van de Mens: Over autonomie, transcendentie en sterfelijkheid,* Amsterdam: Boom.

Hijmans, E., Wester, F., Renckstorf, K. and Scheepers, P. (Eds) (2006) 'De kwalitatieve interviewstudie', *Onderzoekstypen in de communicatiewetenschap,* 2de druk, Alphen a.d. Rijn: Kluwer.

Hoogen van den, T., Hense, E. and Maas, F. (Eds) (2011) 'Elements of a theory about lived spirituality', *Towards a Theory of Spirituality.* Studies in Spirituality, Supp 22, Titus Brandsma Institute, Leuven: Peeters.

Jong de, J. (1947) *Handboek der kerkgeschiedenis,* Utrecht—Nijmegen: Dekker & van de Vegt N.V.

Jonker-Pool, G., de Haes, J., Gualthérie van Weezel, L., Sanderman, R. and van de Wiel, H. (Eds) (2001) 'Kanker: een existentiële opgave', *Psychologische patiëntenzorg in de oncologie,* Assen: Koninklijke van Gorcum, 73–85.

Kallmeyer, H. (1970) *Heilkraft durch Atem und Bewegung,* Heidelberg: Karl F. Haug Verlag.

Kasper, W. *Jesus der Christus,* Mainz: Matthias-Grunewald-Verlag, 1974.

Kolk van der, B. (2014) *The body keeps the score. Brain, mind and body in the healing of trauma,* New York: Penguin Books.

Leget, C., Staps, T., Geer, J.v.d., de Graeff, A., van Bommel, J., van Deijck, R., et al. (Eds) (2010) 'Richtlijn spirituele zorg', *Palliatieve zorg, Richtlijnen voor de praktijk,* Utrecht: Vereniging van Integrale Kankercentra, 637–662.

Lethborg, C., Aranda, S., Block, S. And Kisane, D. (2006) 'The role of meaning in advanced cancer—Integrating the constructs of an assumptive world, sense of coherence and meaning-based coping', *Journal of Psychosocial Oncology,* 24, 1, 27–42.

van Lommel, P. (2007) *Eindeloos bewustzijn,* 14th edition, Kampen: Uitgeverij Ten Have.

Loscalzo, M., Brintzenhofeszoc, K. and Holland, J. (Ed) (1998) 'Brief Crisis Counselling', *Psycho-Oncology,* New York: Oxford University Press, 637–662.

Lossky, V. (1983) *The vision of God,* Crestwood, NY: St. Vladimir's Seminary Press.

Lu K'uan Yu. (1967) *Geheimnisse der chinesischen Meditation,* Zurich, Stuttgart: Rascher Verlag. (Original title: *The Secrets of Chinese Meditation.* London: Rider & Co.)

Lu K'uan Yu. (1970) *Taoist Yoga: The sexual teachings of the ancient Chinese masters,* London: Rider & Co.

Luijpen, W. (1971) *Nieuwe inleiding tot de existentiële fenomenologie,* Utrecht Antwerpen: Spectrum.

MacCulloch, D. (2009) *A History of Christianity,* London: Penguin Books.

Macioca, G. (1989) *The Foundations of Chinese Medicine: A Comprehensive Text for Acupuncturists and Herbalists,* Edinburgh, London, Melbourne, New York: Churchill Livingstone.

Maex, E., Brommer-Fogaras, J., Malinowski, H., Visser, A., Remie, M. and Garssen, B. (Eds) (1998) 'Spiritualiteit in het werken met mensen met kanker', *Psychosociale Begeleiding en Onderzoek bij Kanker en Aids,* Rotterdam: Uitgeverij Marita Meeuwes, 129–132.

Merleau-Ponty, M. (1945) *Phénoménologie de la perception,* Paris: Galimard.

Middendorf, I. (1984) *Der Erfahrbare Atem: eine Atemlehre,* Paderborn: Junfermann Verlag.

Middendorf, I. (2008) *Der Erfahrbare Atem in seiner Substanz,* Paderborn: Junfermann Verlag.

Neimeyer, R. A. and Neimeyer, R. (Ed) (2001) 'Meaning Reconstruction and Loss', *Meaning Reconstruction & the Experience of Loss,* Washington: American Psychological Association, 1–9.

Otto, R. (1923) *Das Heilige: über das Irrationale in der Idee des Göttlichen und sein Verhältnis zum Rationalen,* 11th edition, Stuttgart/Gotha: Verlag Friedrich Andres Perthes.

Ouspensky, L. (1922) *Theology of the Icon. Volume 1,* Crestwood, NY: St. Vladimir's Seminary Press.

Paloutzian, R. F. and Park, C. L. (Eds) (2005) 'Religious conversion and spiritual transformation: A meaning-system analysis', *Handbook of the psychology of religion and spirituality,* New York: Guilford, 331–346.

Pargament, K.I. and Shafranske, A. P. (Ed) (1996) 'Religious methods of coping: Resources for the conservation and transformation of significance',

Religion and the clinical practice of psychology, Washington, DC: American Psychological Association, 215–239.

Patton, M. (1990) *Qualitative Evaluation and Research Methods*, 2nd Edition, Newbury Park, CA: Sage.

Post, R. (1961) *Handboek van de kerkgeschiedenis, deel I*, Nijmegen Utrecht: Dekker & van de Vegt N.V.

Quenot, M. (1993) *De Icoon: Venster op het Absolute,* Tiel : Lannoo/Axios. (original edition Les éditions du Cerf, 1987.)

Rahner, K., Grillmeier, A. and Bacht, H. (Eds) (1954) 'Chalkedon—Ende oder Anfang?', *Das Konzil von Chalkedon,* V l.3, Würzburg: Echter Verlag.

Roselyne de, F. (1978) 'L'Icône de la Transfiguration', *Spiritualité Orientale et Vie monastique, no.23,* Bégrolles en Mauges: Abbaye de Bellefontaine.

Scharschuch, A. (1976) *De ademende mens,* Deventer: Ankh-Hermes.

Schipper, K. (1988) *Tao, de levende religie van China,* Amsterdam: Meulenhoff Informatief. (Original title: *Le corps Taoïste.* Paris: Librairie Arthème, 1982.)

Schrameijer, F. and Brunenberg, W. (1992) *Psychosociale zorg bij kanker,* Utrecht: Nederlands centrum voor Geestelijke volksgezondheid.

Smaling, A. (1987) *Methodologische objectiviteit en kwalitatief onderzoek,* Lisse: Zwets en Zeitlinger.

Staps, T. and Yang, W.(1991) *Psycho-energetische Therapie: Psychosociale begeleiding van kankerpatiënten,* Nijkerk: INTRO.

Strauss, A. (1987) *Qualitative analysis for social scientists,* Cambridge: Cambridge University Press.

Strauss, A. and Corbin, J. (1990) *Basics of qualitative research. Grounded theory procedures and techniques,* Newbury Park: Sage.

Stroebe, M. S., Schut, H. and Neimeyer, R. (Ed) (2001) 'Meaning Making in the Dual Process Model or Coping With Bereavement', *Meaning Reconstruction & the Experience of Loss,* Washington: American Psychological Association, 58.

Turner, V. (1969) *The Ritual Process: Structure and Anti-structure,* Chicago: Aldine pub.

Uden van, M. (1996) *Tussen zingeving en zinvinding. Onderweg in de klinische godsdienstpsychologie,* Tilburg: Tilburg University Press.

Waaijman, K. (2002) *Spiritualiteit: vormen, grondslagen, methoden,* Kampen Gent: Uitgeverij Kok.

Ware, K. and Chirban, J. (Ed) (1996) 'In the Image and Likeness: The Uniqueness of the Human Person', *Personhood—Orthodox Christianity and the Connection Between Body, Mind and Soul,* Westport: Bergin & Garvey.

Wester, F. and Peters, V. (2004) *Kwalitatieve analyse: Uitgangspunten en procedures,* Bussum: Coutinho.

Wester, F. (1995) *Strategieën voor kwalitatief onderzoek*, Bussum: Coutinho.

Wilhelm, R. and Jung, C G. (1985) *Het geheim van de gouden bloem: Een Chinees levensboek,* Deventer: Ankh-Hermes. (Original title: *Das Geheimnis der Goldenen Blüte.* Freiburg i.B.: Walter Verlag, 1931.)

Yang, J. M. (1989) *The Root of Chinese Chi Kung: The Secrets of Chi Kung Training,* Hong Kong: YMAA.

Yang, W. (2021) *Yoga of Courage and Compassion.* Rochester, Vermont: Pub, Inner Traditions/Bear Company.

Yang, W. (2008) 'Spiritualiteit: voorbij de paradox van het individuatieproces', *Individuatie, existentie, psychotherapie*, Tilburg: KSGV, 54–75.

Yang, W., Staps, T. and Hijmans, E. (2010) 'Existential Crisis and the Awareness of Dying: The Role of Meaning and Spirituality', *Omega, Journal of Death and Dying,* 61, 1, 53–69.

Yang, W., Staps, T. and Hijmans, E. (2012) 'Going through a Dark Night, Existential Crisis in Cancer Patients—Effective Coping as a Psycho-spiritual Process embedded in the Vulnerability of the Body', *Studies in Spirituality*, 22, Leuven: Peeters, 311–339.

Yang, W. (2018) *Begrensd en ont-grensd: paradoxen in de veranderende beleving van het Lichaam bij kanker en een geleefde spiritualiteit,* Nijmegen: Valkhof Pers (Ph.D. Thesis, Radboud University, Nijmegen).